MW01265538

LALITAMBA

Number 6

Lalitamba 6
© 2014 Chintamani Books
P.O. Box 131, Planetarium Station
New York, NY 10024
All rights reserved.
ISBN 978-0-9778633-9-6

Lalitamba ISSN 1930-0662 is published annually in the United States by Chintamani Books. The magazine is printed in accordance with the Sustainable Forestry Initiative.

Cover Art by Dietmar Busse, from *Flower Album* (Glitterati, 2006).

Submission Guidelines: Please submit up to five poems or one work of prose per envelope. Include SASE and contact information (name, address, phone, email). Work should be previously unpublished. Address all correspondence to:

Lalitamba
P.O. Box 131
Planetarium Station
New York, NY 10024

Subscriptions are $12 for one year, plus $4.50 postage and handling.

Lalitamba, Inc. is a 501(c)3 nonprofit organization serving the homeless, recovering addicts, and prison inmates. [www.lalitamba.org] *Lalitamba* is in partnership with Refuge, a holistic shelter serving the homeless in New York City. [www.threejewelsrefuge.org] Charitable donations are tax-deductible.

The name for the journal was inspired by a devotional song, "Lalitamba, Lalitamba," sung on a pilgrimage through India. In early 2004, we traveled through the country in an effort to alleviate the suffering that comes with poverty, illness, and plain loss of hope. The journal was founded in November of 2004 by Swamini Sri Lalitambika Devi.

The name "Lalitamba" means Divine Mother. In India, the Divine Mother is often thought of as *jagado dharini,* or "she who supports the universe."

TABLE OF CONTENTS

Poetry

Letters and Prayers. . .

i.
Bless the child that does not
have his own.

ii.
Bless the mother without a
home.

iii.
Bless the people who sleep
beneath the stars at night and
weep for food to eat.

iv.
Bless the soldier as he walks
toward the battlefield; may
he return wearing emblems of
peace.

v.
Bless the preacher, the priest,
and the nun; may they not be
the evil they lambaste.

vi.
Bless this land;
may she grow fruits of
justice and equality, abundantly.

vii.
Bless me—last but not least—
so that I can see strength in
weakness, the eternity of love,
and the power of the pen.

Elvis Alves
New York, NY

The seasons of life—
much joy and laughter.
The seasons of life
came from someone much greater.
Can't you tell from the presents you get?
Come on, come on. Let's hold hands.
Let's give.
Give to the fatherless, joy not pity.
Give to the youths, poor or pretty.
Give to the One, cause together we share,
hoping and praying for another New Year.

Felicia Bratcher
New York, NY

*This journal is
an offering
for liberation.*

Ayaz Daryl Nielsen

BEGINNINGS

Halfway to an ending
I hear the call
of your beginning

Can you meet me here,
halfway? Can you wait
until I arrive at
where you could begin?

Will you wait for me?

Ayaz Daryl Nielsen

UNTITLED

a blackbird
settles
among reeds
for some moments
there is no-
where
I
need
to
be

Eve Powers

WATERFALL

Lead me, Mother,
on narrow paths of deep-bedded green

to mosses drenched with water's fall.
I will shed my clothes on stones,
stand beneath the pummeling roar,
and drink compassion
with my whole skin.

Let me share the rushing plunge
with the little snail
who clings steadfastly
to the flooded rock.
You will quench our common thirst
there, with flowing solicitude.

Eve Powers

DANCE OF TRANSFORMATION

"Quick–give me your hand!"
the Mother cries, as she spins past.
I reach out, take hold—
She sweeps me into the swirl of Her cosmic skirt,
the deafening thunder of Her dancing feet.

In Her shimmering veil,
galaxies eddy into structures of unthinkable size.
In Her flashing gown subatomic particles wink
in and out of existence.
Matter and energy blur.
Events become probabilities.

"The past can't hold you," She calls,
and hurls me across an abyss of fear.

Newborn, I am a star flashing in her skirt,
an ever-recreated universe of possibilities.

James Markay

WOMAN

Woman—grace is.
Elegance is a virtue. To honor is to love
innocently, naturally. *Enso* expressed
is elegance. There is no need for concept,
just the will to endure.
Endure the passion,
passion that gratitude
allows. Woman *mantra*
om. It is a Valentine.
Ego. Sincerity. Justice.
So well you know me.
It is due genesis
that you comprehend me,
a vibration in your presence.
My reality transforms.
You are genuine, woman.

Tara Menon

HER LOTUS PETAL FEET

When I'm in the sanctuary of the prayer room,
when the light from the brass lamps
shines on my face,
when the fragrance of sandalwood fills me,
when the petals shower down from the picture,
when chants reverberate,
when the clash of cymbals
chases away worldly thoughts,
when I feel a maternal presence,
majestic and divine,
bathe me,
promise everlasting bliss—
I surrender to Her lotus petal feet.

Samantha Haines

ROUSED FROM AN EVENING REVERIE

Morris and I share a sleeping bag.

I am here by choice.

We sleep together under the stairs, by choice. There are opportunities for change, but the comfort of companionship sways my reasoning to a desperate place. I could lie under a tree in the park, but the dirt slips under my clothes, sticks to my sweaty arms, and bites at my scalp. This heat dwindles long after the sun has set. We lay on top of the sheath, vulnerable and free. There is time for rumination, but I fatigue. My thoughts collide.

Morris links his arm with mine, and we amble towards the waterfront. I like to watch couples walk.

He plays the accordion. He serenades them with capricious melodies and incomprehensible notes. Coins thrown into plastic cups clash like cymbals marking the climax of an orchestral movement.

I just sit and watch and love them all. Even for this fleeting moment, I appreciate them, and it is mutual.

The music will always begin, but the music will always cease. I listen and feel, as my ears begin to grow.

These men and women, twisted from the same gingerbread dough, they morph. Their joints crack. Crumbs sprinkle into my eyes, barricade my nose. They suffocate me.

And how those gingerbread men and gingerbread women will cheer, when our sleeping bag becomes my casket.

Yet, a young man leans against the gate that marks the water's edge. He stands with a woman who is losing her hair, not in chunks but in individual strands.

Hairs fall out like grains of salt, pressed into the skin of a palm. Slowly, the tiny crystals loosen and drop.

Combs covet them, slowly pilfering youth from the body. They drift across floors, dining room tabletops, and hospital beds. They drop out without declaration and without leaving replacements. You begin to miss them. I miss them. My head has never felt so cold.

Still, I am mesmerized by life.

A child flies in circles, so fast his palm barely meets the bark of the tree he orbits. The flashlight in his hand illuminates an intimate scene that rides the cusp of public interest.

Pass after pass, a secret is unveiled through the inconsistent light. Spidery fingers splay across the cotton-covered stomach of a virgin. There is a brief flash of profile. Heads bow, the soft points of two noses meet, delicately.

My lips part. I inhale the shared, humid air.

Too soon, the small boy skids to a stop. He falls to the ground. His puny chest expands with a deep, exaggerated breath, as he stares at the moon, or the stars, or a plane.

The moment is over, and I too feel heavy and breathless.

The wind rouses me, forces me to stand. I leave Morris and wander down cracked pathways that smell of spoiled beef. Mice skitter.

Eighty years have never passed so quickly.

Without concern, the scene changes.

Consummation bows to the embryo.

I sprout into a touchable entity. I climb from the protective womb, only to be thrown into a deserted road. I raise my head to the sound of a snarling engine. A car hits my innocent body. I soar into the sky, paralyzed but flying! There is no explanation, only blinking, words, touches, slaps, bruises, and blood. There is complete joy, but at the cost of a stretching spine.

It is without reverse. It never stops.

I have been born again, and I have died over and over and over, only to land, changed.

I open my eyes. Now, I am encased in the heat and debris from a recent explosion. A sky is afire, lit like a candlewick.

There's an alley made of poppy sheets. I acquiesce and begin to rest. My back relaxes. I sink through papery concrete.

I'm not ready. Please, I'm not ready.

When the morning comes, I will have surely vanished. Here, right here, this is where it will stop. There isn't a wall or a sign or a cliff, but a complexity of weightlessness.

Hands appear. I feel their touch, and it is boundless. They swim through my stomach, gliding through my throat before uniting in my mind.

Clustered voices sing and cry. I recognize none of them.

Suddenly, Morris speaks. He comforts me with his careful words, "And we'll walk. We'll walk until the road and the sun, conjoin. And we'll be better. Much better. Because we're so much better than they think."

Tayler Klein

ODE TO AN ORANGE

I've decided it's not the rind,
ochre and porous, that peels

from the flesh like snake skin
from a body damp and yielding,

that I love,

nor the poles on either end of the fruit,
empty navels without their mother's cord.

It's not the pulp, waxy and supple between teeth
and tongue, white as sea salt, nor the seeds

suspended like stars in the flesh
of a universe. It's not the slices rounded

like the bellies of boats, bent into the curve
of cupped hands bringing water to lips.

It's not the sharp citrus on the tip of the tongue,
or the perfume that drowns or the juice that trails

down arms, invisible veins. What I love is the way
I pull through the center, fingers through skin

crackling like fire. The fruit is a little Earth, halved,
blazing and ripe, and I hold it—all of it—

in my hands.

Tayler Klein

ORIGINS

Because man is not my maker,

give me back the hollows
of the earth, wombs
water-carved and cool.

Give me back my shape—
my backbone mountain ranges,
my belly, the throbbing red core.

Give me back my name,
and let me write it in constellations
with my own dust and breath.

Give me back the Mother
in God
and let me be made

in Her image—earth-shaped,
earth-colored, earth-tongued
and tied

not to a rib, but to a woman,
to a whole
humming planet.

Jim Richards

ELIJAH

And so the day set over the windy city.
The cars slid into their places of rest
and the people slid into their nights. You,
you were nowhere to be found, and I,
I was looking for you. I stood on the curb
and stared into a puddle of water
glazed with oil. You, you were not in the water,
as God was not in the wind. You were not
in the oil, as God was not in the fire.
Still, I stood there waiting—for an earthquake,
a prophet, a still small voice.

Jim Richards

SCRIPTURE

Breathing October air was like biting
into a cold apple. We'd waited for the taste
all summer. It meant a trip to the canyon
to see the leaves. At the canyon's base

was an iron gate we climbed on and clung to
like the arm of God, as it swung around
one-hundred-eighty degrees and stopped
on a jamb jutting from the earth like the black thumb

of a giant corpse. When we hit it, the force
opened up our bodies and launched our spirits
into the trees. Slowly, they came back to us
and we climbed into the car, and into the canyon.

The narrow canyon road was lined with trees,
and we, with windows down, passed like Moses
through the red, orange, and yellow sea.
"Don't stick your arms out the window,"

our father said. "It's dangerous." And so we did,
and half our torsos too, to touch the flames
flashing on black branches, to feel the slaps
burn our palms and sting our forearms.

It is dangerous. I realize that now. I am the father,
driving with windows down, a cold taste in my mouth,
as my children reach out to test their limbs,
and pass their fingers through the fire.

Gabriele Zuokaite

TALENT

You wake up late, yes when all those awoken by the alarm have already made their coffee. You are lying down and staring at the ceiling, drawing an imaginative trajectory of the fly's flight pattern. You feel like Gulliver, tied down by the Lilliputians with dozens of tiny sturdy ropes. It seems that your bed became the center of the Earth's gravity, and you can't pull yourself out of it.

"Will you stay in your bed forever?"

You ask yourself this, because you can't stand melancholy.

When you don't need to go to work, you concentrate on yourself. You feel as if you've just returned from funeral. I wonder whose?

Peeling your body from those down pillows you sit for a while and look around. Your blue pajamas with teddy bears brighten up the pastels of the loony room. You stand without realizing how weak you are. Your legs move mechanically, carrying you to the restroom. In the mirror, your face looks like it's been powdered white.

You slam the door shut. You sit down on the sill beside the windowpane and watch from your apartment number thirteen window, which is on the fifth floor.

Women scurry and children run.

It is very cold behind the glass, and it is very hot in the apartment. You draw circles with your thin finger on the frosted window.

You touch the glass with your hand, let it rest for a while.

You close your eyes and listen to distant music.

The sounds disperse. They jump around, approach and fade off, and sometimes they freeze.

You wonder what God is busy with in this moment.

Gabriele Zuokaite

BOY'S STORY

When he was five, he wanted to become a pilot. He was flying planes at nights. With eyes wide open, he jumped from one star to another. He was silently humming the little pilot's prayer, until the moon invaded his childish dream and gently stroked him.

When he was ten, he wanted to be a firefighter. He was running in the yard, jumping over the fence, and waving the pretend hose—his father's worn-out muffler. He read too many tales about heroes, about those who are always happy. He wanted to be needed. When his mother was cleaning up his scraped knee, a tear ran down his cheek. He longed for love.

When he was fifteen, he didn't want anything. Finally, he understood that life has its own flow. Tomorrow will happen tomorrow, and today is just today. Thus, he tossed the ball to his friend, his friend passed it back, and he dunked a clean two-pointer.

When he turned twenty, he remembered all the todays and tomorrows he'd talked about as a teenager. Tomorrow finally came. After the university days, he was alone. He strolled around a statue of Oscar Wilde's Happy Prince, a monument to sacrifice. He chose to become a doctor. Now, he spent his days dissecting stale corpses of those who disappeared without a trace.

When he was twenty-five, he got sick. He'd just started his career, but had already gained popularity. Women would drop down on their knees to kiss his feet, when he would save their children. Cleaning ladies did their best to scrub lonely hospital corridors. Unfortunately, disease like air penetrates you to the very core.

Having celebrated his thirtieth birthday, he discovered God. He quit his work, and gave himself away to prayer. He supported those in need and preached. It's not clear how, but the disease was subdued.

When he was thirty-five, he realized that he didn't know love. He packed his things and left. The disease displayed no signs. She found him frozen, at the main entrance. He looked lonely, and she took him in. The woman's hands were warm. Her eyes burned with love. A nun's service could never replace such gentle care. She was the first woman who made chamomile tea for him.

When he turned forty, he rocked his second daughter in tired arms. He returned to work at the hospital and was successful. He seldom found his daughters running around the house. His eyes became heavy, and life's picture became dull.

He turned forty-five and decided to travel around the world with his wife. He enrolled the girls in a preppy school. While traveling, he ate baked chestnuts and sent colorful postcards with happy and beautiful people to his daughters.

Hugging his three beloved women, he celebrated his fiftieth birthday. The disease came back and made him old before his time. Now, he painted with his bare feet.

When he turned fifty-five, his older daughter finished school and started studying law. It hurt him that she didn't become a musician. She used to sing when she lay in the meadow. He'd secretly listened.

By the time he turned sixty, he had buried his wife under the blossoming apple tree. The younger daughter moved in. She wrote about his life. He wasn't famous, or in any way special. He appreciated what he got. He was happy. That was all.

Gabriel Arquilevich

THE OUTSKIRTS *(An Excerpt)*

Cling to your life, and it is your meaning
you see. Follow your version of me,
and we are both alone. You ask for help,
but I cannot solve problems in a dream.
That is what time is for:
Cars collapse, the cat is gone, and Congress
cannot save the nation. Nothing goes well,
even when it seems to, and the escape
is part of your problem. You are not there.

If you believe you are, you are dreaming.
You are here, in the outskirts, deciding
between time and the palm haven.
Choose time, and you will believe
you are unworthy of me.
Forgive, and your version of you
will have nothing to do with me.
I am not disgusted by it.
You are, but so what?
It has no meaning here, in the outskirts,
and so it has no meaning anywhere.

I am here before anything happens.
This is what I mean. Over there, your son
falls and you clench. Your wife speaks
in the wrong tone, and your day crumbles.
You smile at money.

Here, there is only one day, one feeling,
and it goes on forever. You are here,
but your mind is split between time and me,
as though both are true. The outskirts ask you
to choose. Choose time, and time will have its way
with you. With me, everything happens
without distress. What people do
matters less and less, and yet you love them.
Nothing changes. You watch the dream gently.
That is all. You do not give happenings
a truth they do not merit. They come and go,
but the outskirts never change. The outskirts
lead you home, with always the same light.

I show you what is true, everlasting,
lovely, and yours. Nothing over there
can change this purity, no matter what
you do. That is why trying to please me
is a dead end. Doing good gets you
nowhere. In the scaffolding nothing is
true, and so there is nothing good to do.
What others do does not change it,
nor does what happens through them.
This includes your son, your great lesson.

He is the same as you, no matter what
part he plays in the dream. Everyone is.
So, when you fly home with him tomorrow,
and a thousand dangers linger still,
and you are crazy with panic and fear
for his recovery, try to love him
from the outskirts. Try to see him with me.
That is all you can do. Everything else
is of the scaffolding and will not heal
either of you. Your job is to leave him
alone. Leave him alone, and follow me.

Yes, you are happy. There are others
who know, who travel outskirts
of their own. Some stand on bridges,
reaching out to the industrial horizon.
Some circle the holy mountain at dawn;
they return to feed families who
understand their longing for worship.
Others never stray from home, happy
in old armchairs—alone or with friends.

The learning is the same, no matter
what it looks like. You are joined
in the same happiness, promise,
and gathering at the end of time.
You are joined by the same
quiet and remarkable knowledge
that it has happened already.
You are already one, even as you

struggle in the dream. And the gathering
continues, bit by bit—the great return
to love, the desert home, the palm haven.

This is the paradox of the outskirts:
You have arrived, but you are traveling
still, rewinding time to its one moment.
Image by image, you must face what you've made,
until you see it as all the same.
You were born, when you first wandered,
or thought you did.

Good day or bad day, it is all the same.
That is why your son is your salvation.
If you are here, and I am not a dream,
then he is safe. There is nothing to fear,
even if he backslides, even if you lose him.
He reminds you of me,
and so he has recovered already.

In the scaffolding, this is blasphemy.
Everything testifies to loss and death.
The lower mountains hold the evidence,
and it is this you must travel through, now.
All of time and place and all of memory
are condensed in this
space that only seems to be.
It is not real. That is what you are
learning. That is what you are afraid of.
That is why I am here. That is why you are blessed.

Philip Kobylarz

OUR LADY OF THE GUARD

You see them, wherever you go. Sunday mornings, on Broome Street, they walk arm in arm. He wears a trench coat and carries the *Times* under his elbow. She's telling him something private and unimportant, and hanging onto a leash that harnesses a nondescript mutt. The dog sniffs at every wad of garbage and stain on the sidewalk. All three are oblivious to the steady drizzle, to the bare branches of maple trees.

Or they're on Michigan Avenue. They drink steaming cups of coffee out of waxy paper cups. They smile and walk slowly over the bridge. They gaze through its eroding segments to see the still green river.

In early afternoon snow, they're silently thinking each other's thoughts.

Come evening, they're at the beach after sunset. Theirs is the only car in the empty parking lot that has become a gathering point for hungry seagulls. A flick of a lighter illuminates their heads, for an instant. Radio voices slip from the opened window. The surf churns foam, empty bottles, cigarette butts, and strands of seaweed up onto the stones, darkened where they touch water.

The traffic is heavy at this time of night.

I wait impatiently on the roadside. I am ready to jaywalk. Soon, the soccer stadium will be filled with rowdy fans. Already, some race from neighborhood bars to get the best parking and seats available. It's obvious who they are by the speed at which they're driving. They honk out the local team's song, as they pass beachside restaurants. *Doot dadoot doot doot doot.*

Because it's winter, Marseilles isn't as crowed as it normally is. That's why I'm out walking tonight. There's an edifying solitude to being in prime locations at the wrong time—the abandoned bars in ski towns during long summers, the barren streets of Phoenix seared by afternoon sun, or anywhere in Los Angeles when it rains.

Marseilles has erected a statue at its main intersection. I have an hour to make it up the hill to the cathedral.

In my backpack, I have all I need for my pilgrimage: a notebook and a bottle of water.

The hillside dwellings are painted the color of salmon. Their adobe walls are lined with colorful pieces of broken bottle, in green, blue, and lacquer brown. Sharp edges have been dulled by erosion. The leveling power of the wind is a force in these parts.

The hill's two-hundred-metre elevation seems innocuous. Still, it has me breathing hard three-quarters of the way up. This terrain is semi-arid. The city clings to steep outcroppings of calcite. The landscape is like desert, but pines spring up here and there.

I pass a garden of wild vegetation bounded by yuccas.

I pass a woman carrying a bag of oranges. She says something about the wonderful view that awaits me. Her hair is dyed with henna. She descends the hill in high heels.

The Moorish spires of the cathedral reach into a blindingly bright sky. They are stained with the gunfire of Germans who once attempted to take the citadel.

As a matter of pride, the locals let it be known that this part of the country has never been under a Teutonic yoke. Every crack and fissure of the edifice emphasizes its longevity.

When I reach the hilltop, I am surprised to see a group of older Arabs as the only visitors. The men are dressed in grey jackets with their white *chechias*. The women wear resplendent *djellabas* lined with gold lamé. They take the stairs slowly, because of their swollen ankles.

When they reach the top, they look over the sea and point out towards the clouds where Algeria might be. Or Morocco. Or Tunisia.

An Egyptian ocean liner steadily crosses the water. From this great height the labyrinth of the city becomes apparent. The tight matrix of red-tiled buildings below us begins to make sense.

A couple holds each other, speaking quietly. They are unaware of the futility of traffic and the bellowing ships. They await what is theirs that evening—the sun falling into the sea.

Once I enter the cathedral, I no longer wonder why believers of another faith, like myself, would be here.

The ornate interior diffuses such small irony.

Like an art gallery, there are paintings hung on the walls, mobiles of wooden ships strung from the vaulted ceiling, and mosaics of the most stunning colors tiling the floor.

The paintings were done by locals, who had been released from perilous circumstance through the grace of divine intervention, or by children.

There is one of a downed Sopwith Camel with its pilot lying dazed over the target symbol on the wing. A radiant Virgin watches over the scene. Heaven shines in the upper-right-hand corner.

Another is of a cat flung to the side of the road by a car, yet miraculously alive, the red tag of its tongue sticking out.

There are paintings of clipper ships on stormy seas; of bus crashes in the country; of hospital invalids with smiling faces. The Virgin looks over them all. She is arrayed in colors of glory.

A barely audible whispering brings me back from my trance. A small woman bent over in the front pews catches my attention. She is busy saying the Rosary.

When I see the shawl covering her head, I know who she is. I know her by name. Angèle.

I am her sister's grandson, long unknown to her. I'd found her name in my grandmother's address book, years ago.

Just two days ago, I'd called and explained as best I could who I was, and that since I was in this part of the country, I would like to meet her.

Now, she is patiently waiting, steeped in a faith I do not share.

I approach.

"Hello Madame, let me introduce myself," I begin.

She embraces me. "You are the spitting image of your mother. It is so good to finally meet you."

I offer to take her to lunch in the cafeteria nearby, but she refuses. She tells me that we will have lunch at her home.

On the bus ride, she points out the houses of neighbors and people she knows. There is the mansion of a Christian Lebanese general who seeks asylum in the city. The ornate house is guarded by militia men. It is separated from the street by moveable iron barricades. It leans on a crag at the sea's edge.

There is the apartment of Edward, who lost his arm in the war. He comes over on Thursday nights to drink whiskey and play cards.

There is where Lorraine lives, with her three sisters. They cook meals for the nuns in the Orthodox convent.

Her own house is a tiny affair that is more garden than living quarters. She apologizes for the absence of the carnations and gladioli that regularly surrounded the place. It is winter.

Inside, her son Aldo greets me, as does a lethargic black cat named Fishbone.

Angèle makes soup for Aldo and me, as if we are both regular lunch-time visitors. She tinkers around the kitchen and sings a tune under her breath.

Aldo asks me many questions.

We tell our stories between mouthfuls of soup, then bread, then fish, then salad, then cakes.

When the food finally stops arriving, Angèle sits down next to me. She simply smiles.

I asked her how she had come here and why.

She begins.

"When I was a little girl, about fifteen or sixteen, I worked on a farm. I was in charge of the daily chores, you know, watering the chickens and the ducks, taking hay to the cows, collecting eggs, feeding the goats, combing the horses' manes.

"There was another worker there named Gregor who was of the marrying age and who was, although I didn't know it at the time, seeking me as his prospect. He wasn't an ugly man, but he was large and burly. He had lost an eye, when a stubborn mule decided to kick him in the head, rather than move.

"One day, this Gregor wanted to help me fetch hay for the cows. It had been raining like the dickens for three days, but on this day, the rain was sparse, like a mist. The thunderheads rumbled in the distance, though the wind was pushing them away from our neck of the woods, and the skies were a lighter grey than they had been.

"I let him assist me, because haying the cows was not much fun. Although I was a strong girl, the hay was scratchy, getting into my blouse and hair, and heavier than you might think.

"He followed me up the ladder to the loft, where the hay was stored. We began pushing clumps of it off the loft to the floor. We were sweating like pigs, because it is much warmer at the heights of the barn than at the bottom, where there are doors.

"He removed his shirt.

"Meanwhile, I stopped every few minutes to wipe the sweat from my brow and eyes. I joked with him, saying that it must be easier for him to work hard. The sweat could only go into one of his eyes, so he shouldn't have to stop as often as I do.

"When I turned to acknowledge my bit of humor, I saw him standing there, looking at me. Quite mechanically, he pulled at the rope holding his burlap pants onto his waist, and let me say, he did not look tired at all. He was straight up like a pitchfork. Breathing like an animal, he took me by the arms and threw me into the bundle of hay.

"I was a young girl. I didn't know what was going to happen, although I had some idea of what was taking place.

"Once, father told me to throw ice cold water from the trough on a stray dog who got stuck in a barn cat. Both of them were wailing together in the grain house.

"Gregor had much the very same look in his eye as that poor old dog did.

"I said, 'No, no. Gregor, don't treat me like an animal of the barn. You can do whatever you like, but please go get a blanket, even if it is the old blanket we put under the horse's saddle. The hay and sharp pieces of straw may cut me. Father will ask me about the cuts when I bathe myself in the tub tonight.'

"He held me so close that the sweat from his forehead dropped into my eyes. Everything became blurry, but I could hear his breath. His tongue was like an arrow being held on a bow, about to be unleashed from its quiver.

"After a moment of thought, he agreed.

"Unable to re-tie the knot of rope fastened to his pants, he let them fall to his ankles. He hobbled down the ladder.

"He took the blanket from a peg on the wall.

"When he was almost to the loft, I pushed the ladder out as far as I could with my bare feet.

"Gregor grabbed at it with his hands.

"With much exertion, he managed to balance on the ladder.

"I thought that it might fall back onto the loft and that I would be raped. I thought I might become pregnant and have to marry this awful man. A terrible future played out like a moving picture in my mind.

"But when his pants tore in half from between his ankles, he looked down, and the ladder toppled backwards. He fell to the ground on his back.

"I yelled for help. Poppa came into the barn.

"I said that Gregor fell, because I accidentally pushed the ladder away from the loft with a stroke of the pitchfork.

"Gregor was moaning. He lay in the dirt with the rags of his pants around his ankles.

"We never discussed the event ever again.

"It turned out that Gregor had only broken his shoulder bone and some ribs. He would return to our farm in the autumn.

"I knew that something terrible would happen to me, if we were both to be working in a field, beyond a call to the house. I knew I had to leave.

"Your grandmother had saved enough money to take the boat to America. Before she left, she gave me the name of a family living in Paris who had posted a work notice at the university. These people needed a maid to keep the house and care for the children.

"I wrote them a letter, and they offered me the job. So I was off to Paris.

"It was a much better life. I lived in a big house. I would only have to go to the street to find milk, bread, and fine cheeses.

"The man I worked for was a government official. He paid me well.

"The children were darling. I was very happy.

"Then, the Germans took the city. The family I worked for had to leave. Without an explanation, they told me I should get out of the city and go far away to be safe. They were moving to another country, but they wouldn't tell me where. Their secrecy was to ensure my own safety.

"I packed what little I had. With a friend who'd been a cook in a restaurant that the Germans shut down, I went to find work elsewhere."

At this point, Angèle's speech begins to wax more and more into an accent. It becomes hard for me to understand her story.

Aldo helps by translating phrases here and there.

Her eyes begin to gloss over. As she speaks, she stares at the embroidered pattern on the tablecloth.

"It so happened that the Germans briefly controlled the hospital here in the southern part of the country. When they left, the Italians took over but soon abandoned the place. Eventually, for reasons beyond my knowledge, the British took control. We were offered jobs doing the laundry and whatnot, but we had to hitchhike down here from Paris.

"On the way, we stopped in a small town. I don't remember the name of it, only that it was large enough to have a zoo.

"We used cloth bags to carry what little luggage we could take. These bags doubled as blankets. We made our beds in an empty zoo cage that had previously housed wolves from the forests of Bavaria. It still smelled of them. Their droppings lay around like loaves of moldy bread.

"I barely slept that night, because of the noise the rats made. I kept waking, thinking that there was a solitary wolf they had forgotten to remove, a wolf hiding in the corner and ready to attack us at any moment.

"In the morning, we were awakened by men's voices and loud noise. One of the horses had died, and the workers were cutting it into rations. I saw the body of this lovely creature disassembled, as if it were a broken toy.

"I remember that ride through the country, through the farmland that turned from rows of corn into lines of black, wiry grapevines. These green hills that bleached to white became my country.

"When we finally arrived here, there was a notice posted in the hospital. If one could raise a certain amount of money, a visa could be issued to go to America.

"My dear friend who was younger than I didn't have enough money. I gave her the rest of mine, from my days working as a maid. The next day, I said my goodbye to her at the port. I have never seen or heard from her again.

"At the grocery store, I found an ad for a room. The landlord explained that it would have electricity in a week or so.

"Despondent as I was, I moved in immediately. I cooked my meals outside using wood; I washed my clothes down the hill in the sea. That room was in the house next door."

Aldo breaks in saying, "And in that week, he did provide the electricity. The landlord, you see, is my father."

We burst into laughter.

But Aldo soon becomes solemn. He explains that his father is quite sick and is staying in the very hospital that was Angèle's passport to freedom. The beginning of her life and the sad chapter that is now unraveling are to be found in the same location. The hospital is just up the hill, overlooking the turquoise Mediterranean.

"We would go to the horse races, even the bullfights when they had them. Or we would just walk along the beach and watch the hills turn orange at day's end. Now, they won't even let me bring him meals. I can only see him for a few hours a day."

She begins to cry.

Outside, it is dark. The features of the Black Madonna hanging near the window can no longer be discerned.

We exchange telephone numbers and addresses.

As I prepare to depart, Angèle offers me a room.

I tell her that I have rented one on the other side of town. I promise that the family in America will make contact as soon as possible.

They both thank me. Angèle gives me a biscuit for the bus ride back. Aldo hugs me, as if I were his long-lost son.

I don't want to leave.

Fishbone the cat follows me as far as the front gate.

I close the lock and wave goodbye.

I catch the bus on the top of the hill, near the tall hospital building that stands with most of its lights on. The bus is empty, except for a couple who hold onto each other, as if the destination they long for is sleep. His leather jacket creaks they move.

You see them everywhere you go, carrying bread home from the baker or watching television together in a dimly lit apartment, levels above the main street. They travel to foreign countries together or hold jobs in the same office. They talk of vacations they once shared in the mountains or the times they learned how to ride mopeds along narrow alleys. They share the quotidian intimacies of the day. They leave their shoes, stepping on each other at the door. Their clothes are intertwined in the hamper. Theirs are the secrets of how they met and fell in love and how they let this love narrate the all-too-short story of their lives.

When we reach my temporary block, I signal for a stop. I still hold the biscuit Angèle has given me in the warm hollow of my pocket.

The doors hiss open, and the bus driver turns.

I wonder where the young couple is staying. If they live in this neighborhood, their apartment can't be too far from where I am going.

Elisavietta Ritchie

TIGER UPSTAIRS
ON CONNECTICUT AVENUE
for Taj Johnson

"He is crouching here. Pat him."

We swirl our intricate patterns
over invisible white-tufted ears.

A feline leaps at fluttering hands
for his diversion and ours, aware
that fingers are not genuine butterflies.

My mind flutters back to orange-and-
brown butterflies clustered on mud
by the jungle river in Taman Negara.

Nights, a Malay tiger encircled our hut,
might have leapt through windows not
screened, shutters imperfectly hinged.
One swipe of his paw could rip away
the mosquito netting over our bunks.
Every morning we found tiger prints.

Our palms stroke air. We are aware that
this tiger could snatch our fingers, five at a bite.

Taj switches venues. "Imagine
we're in a cell now, fire in the pit,
a pot of water is boiling, vapor—"

"Where's the tiger?" I ask.
"Forget the tiger," he says.

You can't just dismiss a tiger.
The tiger is here, in the steam,
grooms orange-black-white fur,
cleans whiskers, claws, teeth.

He tips the pot. The water cools.
His tongue furls to a funnel, laps.
Belly-up, he rolls in a puddle.

Tigers don't mind being wet:
One paddled behind our raft,
as we poled that brown river.

It is hard to focus on ritual patterns,
with a tiger patrolling the premises.

I recall that envoy from Okinawa
nabbed as a spy in China, thrown
into a cell with a tiger unfed a week.

Guards peered through the bars stunned
to observe their captive perform marital arts
while the tiger watched, and soon fell asleep.

The prisoner shared rations of rice and tea
with the beast, and practiced his dances.

At the week's end they released him. And his tiger?

His tiger trails me down the stairs
to the avenue, the whole way home,
leaves prints on my Ningxia carpet,
orange-and-black hairs on my bed.

Elisavietta Ritchie

A DIFFERENT JUNGLE STORY

We'll walk this jungle
forever. No parents goad.
Only captors.

We who never dared touch,
are now bound together. Ropes
lash our ankles and wrists.

At least they untied
our blindfolds.
We can see—

We see trees, stumble
on banyans, and grab saplings
to scale muddy slopes.

Jacob's Ladder
leads to another ridge, down
to another ravine.

Leaves mottle the sky.
Sunlight filters down. Night
turns phosphorescent.

Old logs become patches
of moonlight. Worms glow green.
Sparks zip up the night.

Who knows that we're missing,
from somewhere? We have crossed
borders with no customs.

This war moves
without shadow or tracks,
though at dawn we see tiger prints.

The war forces us to trudge on. We
don't know where we are going,
where we have been.

We slip on wet leaves. They
yank us into monsoons. Torrents
are rain we can drink.

Trails disappear into logs.
Logs bridge a stream. If I
slip, we both fall.

All swim thick rivers.
All bleed from leeches. Blood,
crimson as ginger, blooms.

I place one ginger
bloom in your fingers. You notice
no sign and recall—

eloquent once, now
mute. Their blow to your
head knocked out speech.

You are not
wholly amnesic. In streams
you seem to pray.

They slap me to silence.
Who could overhear rainbowed birds,
monkeys, millipedes?

Guards whisper in no tongue
I decipher, though they
know commands and oaths in mine.

We lose weight daily,
while guards share bananas, rice,
dried fish, and chilies.

They roast a squirrel
and gnaw the bones clean. We eat in
silence, watched by rifles.

I watch you. Across
tables our eyes once held
brave conversations

that our mouths dared not speak. Now
between us are vines, toadstools,
orange butterflies, and mud.

At least they keep us
leashed like two hounds, with six
feet of rope between us.

I hide for a moment
beyond a banyan. You
pretend not to see.

You don't. They broke your
glasses, and maybe your mind. They
aren't sentimental—

unlike your friends who
schemed we be alone in that
hut where they brought us.

To collect fishermen's
tales will take days. We followed
figures flowing, tide

down the beach, until they
vanished. Did your friends
arrange the ambush?

Do they cover our
absence with their inventions?
No, your friends protect you.

Our captors may know
your importance for barter.
Might I have some worth?

Who we are may not be clear.
Papers were taken,
who knows where, or to whom.

Towns in the hills are burned
to the ground. Jungle
devours old camps.

We lose traces and traits,
as we move like
migrating creatures.

You don't know I'm here.
But at night, guards watch
as we move close for warmth.

Bound hands still caress.
Bound legs encircle, and we
become conjoined twins.

This dawn, your lips are
moths on my ear. Keep playing
the game. Understand

our freedom. Danger
is not here in the jungle.
We break camp, march on.

Stephen Booker

TILT-ZEN CAMPAIGN STICKERS

It's only because I again have
nothing to do that you find another
one of these breaking upon your day—
an ineffably blue downbeat moth
held in abeyance, in that hideaway
back in the I-nearly-forgot spot.

From here on you're not offered a choice.

Its, without an apostrophe, is mine.

Date, off its tree, vanishes—palmed off.

With but a little masked credulity,
the nature of thirst is to drink
cool, sweet water. Crocodiles
caress the surface of this learning.

Of fire or water, the old rules apply.

Flames burn. Water is still or churns, sweetly.

Butter in the mouths of the pious rich
melts the same as on a dragon's tongue.

Because of nothing, or because of nature,
it is reasonable not to think
too much about the candidates or sausage.

Drinks are for everyone holding a skull.

Fire burns in every hearth beneath these dark stars.

R.I. Sutton

THE SENNACHIE

The sun gave its first light to the water from beyond a scroll of parchment-coloured cloud. It gleamed in streams of golden ink on lead, an unfathomable script upon the waves.

Over the face of it now passed a boat, a rowboat bleached, briny, and peeling.

Sitting on its thwart was an old man. His hair was the colour of bone, his face of wet sand. As he heaved the oars, his skin rolled over sinew in easy motion with the sea. Resolved were his movements, and sharp was his eye, as he cast it to the east.

To the east, he had glimpsed a telltale glitter, and it was towards this that he toiled, with something like gold fever in his eyes.

When he came at last to the place, he set the oars and leaned over the side to peer into the depths. It was barely there—that shadowed something—little more than a shifting incandescence. Pulling a sack from the boat, he drew out three wooden tubes. These he locked one inside the next to form a long, whip-like pole. After threading the line, he stood, squinting into the sun. With a swift movement akin to dance, he cast. In that second, as the sun caught his lure like a burning star and ignited his halo of hair, he seemed something more than a hunched and gray old man.

He settled back into the boat. His eyes were fixed upon the fugitive horizon. As his gaze followed the horizon, he opened his mouth and sang.

The golden ocean lulls my tired eyes,
as from above the heavens shine their light,
and air and ocean meet at edge of sky.
So God's two hands, two worlds in Him unite.
As fisherman between them I will roam,
the port of two worlds promised as my home.

Reclined in the boat as he was, he seemed an old knight nestled in his coffin, with fishing pole in place of a sword. He closed his eyes, and here he stayed, even as another fishing boat and its flock of scavenging gulls appeared against the sky, even as it crept towards his little vessel, filling the air with the scent of fish and the engine's churning roar. It circled him once, like a crow scouting game, before drifting to a stop beside him.

A man leaned over the stern. "Are you alright?" he yelled.

The fisherman opened his eyes. "Yes," he said, smiling up at the man. "Are you?"

The trawler frowned. "You're a long way from the shore, Mister," he said. "Do you need a lift back?"

"I am fishing," the old man replied.

"Yes," said the trawler with a laugh. "I can see that you're angling with a cane pole in the middle of the ocean—and in a rowboat, no less. This isn't Lake Pleasant, Mister—it's dangerous out here. You could end up as shark food."

"Such is the lot of the fisherman," the old man said with a sad smile.

"Fisherman!" said the trawler. "How long have you been out here?"

"Since before dawn," the old man replied.

"And how many fish have you caught?" he asked, eyeing the empty boat.

"If the number of fish the fisherman makes, the monger must be the envy of all the sea," said the old man.

The trawler sighed and glanced at his watch. "Look, Mister," he said, "how's about you climb aboard, and we tow your boat back in? I'll even shout you an ale afterwards."

The old man's eyes did not leave the water. "I have not got my catch," he said.

"That's no matter," said the man with a flick of his hand. "I'll give you a couple'a mine to bring back to the Missus. She'll be none the wiser." He nodded his head towards the deck, towards the slippery masses of fish piled there.

"No, thank you," he said. "As my father said to me and his father to he—'A fisherman true will court the sea, until she sees fit, his bride to be.'"

The trawler stared down at the old man, running his fingers through his beard. For a long moment, the two men gazed at each other across the waves. The sound of the water rose between them, and the squall of the gulls accentuated the silence.

Abruptly, the man cleared his throat and turned back to the wheel. "Right," he said, starting the engine. "Suit yourself."

With a churn and a roar he was gone, the bickering of the gulls drifting behind to be battered and drowned by the waves.

* * *

The sun reached its zenith and began its descent. Still, the fisherman's line did not move. The water continued its surging dance, and the sea stretched around him, but the man did not look to adjust his course, nor did he move as yet another boat emerged from the sky. This vessel was white. It glided over the waves swiftly, like a swan.

A group of men stood upon its deck, and such was the bristling of their rods that the craft seemed more a battalion than a pleasure boat. Above the hum of its engine, voices rang out over the water.

"Hey Bob," a man yelled, "there's that fellow the trawler was talking about on the radio!" The craft veered towards him and came to a stop beside the little vessel. From its hull, a cluster of faces peered down at the old man, as an audience would at a clown.

"Hey—you there," called one of the men. "What are you doing?"

The old man's expression did not change, as he looked up at them. "I am fishing," he said.

An explosion of laughter rolled over the waves.

Another face pushed forward. "Where's your catch?"

The fisherman smiled. "I have no catch, yet," he replied.

Their laughter resounded again, as raucous as the cackling of gulls. One voice rose above the rest—"What do you think he's fishing for, Frank—a mermaid?"

An arm snaked over the edge, tipping an amber stream of beer into the sea. "I know what your problem is, old man— You forgot to get her drunk first!"

A new face pushed between the others. "Go easy, boys," it said. "Obviously, the fellow's out of sorts."

"Hey, Mister," he said, "what're you angling for— snapper, whiting, bream?"

"Something much rarer than that," said the fisherman.

"Striped bass?" said the man.

The fisherman did not reply.

"Well, what bait're you using?" he asked.

"No bait," said the old man, "a lure."

"A lure?" said the man with a laugh. "You know, you're supposed to cast a lure."

"This lure is different," replied the fisherman, the smile in his eyes stopping short of his mouth. "It's not made to fool the fish, but to entice him."

The man frowned. "I haven't heard of anything like that. Is it new?"

"Oh no," said the fisherman. "In fact it's old—very old. It came to me through my father—through his death. But I'm sure you fellows don't have time to listen to an old fool's tales."

The men stared down at him from their wall, their feet shuffling, their smiles turning stale on their lips. Finally, one spoke up. "Well," he said, "what happened?"

The old man adjusted his seat, shifting his hands on the pole. "There was a time," he said, "when the ocean became barren. The selkies—those women of the sea who had, for so long, stolen lone fishermen from their boats—disappeared.

Even the gulls stopped their squabbling and flew to the lakes." He looked to the west, as though watching a diminishing flock of birds.

"The people began to starve for want of fish. The only thing left for them to do was something that had been forbidden, years before."

"What—gamble?" laughed one of the men.

"Dive for pearls," said the old man. "It was a dangerous business, that," he said, fixing them with a grave eye. "The ocean is jealous of her jewels and buries them deep." His gaze drifted back to the horizon.

"So," said one of the men. "What happened?"

The old man roused himself. As he spoke, his eyes glimmered. "There was a sleeping volcano beneath the sea. Old folk called it Tiamat's Mouth. Very few had seen it, but those who had told of rocks aclutter with pearl-filled clams.

"But these weren't just any pearls," he said, raising a hand. "These were the most precious of all—perfectly round and so full of luster that they glowed in the dark."

"I don't believe it," scoffed one of the men.

"You may believe it or not," said the fisherman, "but it was for tales like these that my father was willing to girdle himself with rocks and dive into the depths with nothing more than a pickaxe and a string bag."

The men stood silent, their eyes half-closed against the water's glare, their hands gripping the railing.

"I was there when he dove into those depths. I waited with the men as the seconds turned into minutes, and the minutes dragged into a painful eternity." He shook his head. "They tried hauling him up by the rope tied around his waist,

67

but no matter how they heaved and hoed, the rope wouldn't budge." His eyes disappeared into the creases of his face.

"I dived in without thinking," he said. "I followed his line all the way down into the deep."

The slap of the waves on the hull set up a pensive rhythm. Far overhead, a lone gull squalled.

"So what was it like?" asked one of the men, the interest in his eyes belying the monotone of his voice.

The old man looked down at his hands. "It was like swimming through night, a darkness shot through with kind of directionless light. I can only compare it to a dream, for it was closer to that than all of this—" He cast his arm in a gesture encompassing sky, sea, and boat. "And there, weighing the end of the line like a dead fish was my father, his hand caught in the maw of the biggest clam I had ever seen."

"What did you do?"

"Well, my eyes weren't much for seeing down there, but I knew he was gone from this world, and that trying to pick that thing from the rocks would be like trying to shift a blower with a butterfly net. My lungs were exploding, and my limbs were as stiff as dead mullets from the cold, so I left his body and swam for my life." He leaned back in the boat.

"It was full dark before the thing got hungry and opened its maw—before we could drag my father up. We laid him out on the deck, and as we did, we found something we hadn't expected. Clutched in his hand, so tight that they had to break his fingers to get at it, was the roundest, most flawless pearl we had ever seen, shining in his palm like the moon."

The fisherman's eyes passed over them, holding each man, until each man looked away.

"What did you do with it?" asked one of them. "Did you sell it?"

"Oh no," said the fisherman, "I kept it."

"But why?" said another. "That gem could've made you rich."

"Oh, but it did," replied the old man. "You see, I could not have been better off had my father hauled an entire chest of pirate's loot from the floor. This pearl was special. The old folk called it a sea charm. Only a few had ever been found."

"What was so special about it?" the man asked.

"It brought great fortune to whoever possessed it."

"Like it did for your father?" said another, rousing a chorus of laughter.

The fisherman waited for them to finish. "That depends entirely on how you see death," he said. "There's an old sailor's verse that my father said summed up both the most honourable life and the most dignified death.

To be taken by one's mistress,
but to leave a happy wife,
to see one's ship fully sailed—
this is the compassed life.

The men glanced at each other, their faces mottled with annoyance, confusion, and doubt. Their feet shuffled on the deck.

"I kept the pearl and took my father's place as fisherman. Never again did we want for anything, for the fish returned to the sea, and so long as we needed it, my catch was good."

"But what about the pearl?" asked one.

"Oh, I have it still," replied the fisherman with a smile. "In fact, it's suspended from a line not four fathoms beneath your feet."

"What?" cried the men, their bodies jostling, their faces wilting with disbelief.

"Do you expect us to believe," said one of the men, "that you've got a rare gem submerged beneath the water on a fishing line?"

The fisherman did not reply.

Another face pushed forward. "If it's true," he said, "you'll show us."

The old man shook his head. "Alas," he said, "I cannot."

"But why? We won't steal it, if that's what you think."

"It's not thievery that worries me," said the fisherman. "It has always been that once I sink my line, I do not bring it up again until it is taken."

The men groaned and jeered from the vessel, and the fisherman settled his gaze on the water once more. He did not move as they yelled, even as a tin can shot towards him and bounced into his boat. Eventually the engine buzzed into life and the craft began its retreat, the men's yells made hollow by the rising wind.

* * *

The sun cooled into a copper disk, as it sank toward the ocean. Now, with the day's end, the sky began its awakening. Clouds smeared the horizon, speeding the dominion of night. The wind ceased its play for hunger, to lick the crests of the waves.

A light flickered against the swell, and a flash of lightning revealed it to be yet another boat, moving fast. Lurching like a crazed horse, it sped toward the rowboat. Its engine whirred desperately.

A man in a great black coat leaned starboard as it passed, his face a white blur in the diminishing light. His voice faded and flared on the wind. "…Storm coming…no time for pleasure fishing…are you crazy?"

Then, like an apparition, he was gone, swallowed in the pitch of a monstrous wave.

Crawling from his nest in the boat, the old man took a seat on the thwart. He steadied his line carefully. He locked his pole in a notch, so that it stood over the water. Then, he took up the oars and began to guide the boat. As he swept between the waves, he sang.

> Southern wind, herder of the sky;
> O mighty force, beyond both eye and limb—
> Your steeds are loose, and ocean-bound they fly.

Straying clouds, steeds of southern wind;
your master cries his seeking from on high,
and wields his whip to bring you home to him.

With lowered hook, I must not give my ground,
though storm may choose my boat to sweep around.

Bracing his feet against the hull, the fisherman guided the boat over slick, swelling waves, through avalanches of foam. The ocean sizzled, as rain swept towards him, plastering his hair to his forehead.

The sea surged and crashed around him. As his little vessel teetered and shuddered and dived, he rode its back.

His eyes were wide, his mouth a tight knot in the tangle of his beard. Scanning the waters, he seemed to be listening to a melody strung between the waves.

When the end of his fishing pole suddenly bent like a bow, he broke from his watch, dropped the oars, and scrabbled for the line.

Too late, he turned to retrieve them, only to stare as they slipped from the boat and dipped into the waves. He stood, grasping the pole, watching the oars sweep away. Then, his line gave another sharp pull, and he fell.

He teetered over the water, the boat seesawing dangerously close to the waves, the pole slipping to a finger hold in his grasp. Adjusting his grip, he braced himself against the hull, and with a weary heave, regained his footing. He steadied the little vessel with his weight.

Just as he recovered his seat on the thwart, a great wave closed over him, filling the boat with water that frothed like ale. The boat rode low on the waves now, its sides barely free of the surf.

The lightning cut the waves out in knife points. The rain dashed like blue spears.

He sat with eyes closed, a still point in a world of motion. His hands shook on the pole. His knuckles went white, and the tendons in his shoulders sagged.

But then, it came again—a quick, firm tug upon the line. Opening his eyes, the old man blinked to clear them. He ran a hand over his brow, to dispel his weariness as well as the rain. His jaw grew sharp beneath his beard, and the fever returned to his eyes. He jammed his feet against the prow and gave the pole three firm tugs.

The fish responded, throwing its weight against the line. The fisherman wrestled his elbows to his hips, the muscles taut in his arms. The little boat began to move.

With one last rumble, like iron on stone, the storm passed, a smudge of dirty gray against the north horizon. The wind eddied, as the waves melted into rippling downs, the torrents into snowy fields. Through these fields now sailed the old man in his boat, a fair breeze blowing at his back. His line zigzagged ahead of him, strong and taut, with beads of water glowing on its length.

As the night rolled her mantle for morning, and the tides changed from blue-black to gray, the little boat sailed east, drawn by a fish through a quicksilver sea.

The dawning light expanded, at first just mist, then swelling to a canticle of mauve, crimson, and pink. Girding the horizon, so that it might have been nothing more than a mass of purple cloud, stretched a land of mountains and glinting streams. Sea mist hung low like a cloak. As the sun passed through, the whole country emerged haloed in light.

The little boat drew nearer, and nearer still, and as it did, the land became harmonious, like a song with each new voice raised. First, the violet heads of the mountains, and then, the twisting ribbon of beach. And as the old man listened, the weariness gone now from his eyes, other things came to him—the hiss of the waves on the sea shore and the whispering of the trees.

His boat passed now into the path of the sun on the waves. With the warmth came the lush scent of greenery. His skin tingled in the flush of dispelling mist. And when the sun surmounted the mountains, throwing the land into light, every leaf of every tree and every grain of sand sparkled with an inner fire.

Jane Galin

AWAKENING

You awaken in the night to another darkness,
the older one that rivers travel,
quiet and uncrowded,
and you know that after all the many years,
your failures have abandoned you.
You do not ask why.
Without them life is simple,
is only love sharing what food it has,
a loaf of bread,
a bowl of rice,
making its table
anywhere upon the earth.
It will be so.
You and your friends,
your dear ones,
hands open,
as much to give as to receive,
feed and are fed, delightfully.
Through you God tastes.
When the stranger comes,
his hunger a silent call,
you are not frightened.
Your hands do not close.
You turn,
instinctive to the warmth in him,
hidden deep in the chill

of the body's need,
the life no one may have met before,
and you widen the circle to include him.
Along with bread,
you lay a smile
like scented branches
at the threshold of his heart,
and through you God feasts.

Awake in the night,
you listen for the river,
for the sound that never began
and has no end,
elusive.
You reach for it.
You try to press a song
from wordless peace,
and you cannot.
You try and cannot at all,
and still no failure wants you.

Jane Galin

A STRANGER'S SMILE

A man told me how
a stranger's smile saved his life.
He had gone out, he said,
to walk in a park,
to try to take hope from the rooted trees,
or the all-allowing water of the lake,
or a noisy bird,
or the sky,
whole and abiding,
a sky unconvinced by clouds—
anything to stay him,
so forsaken was his soul.

He said that in the live black
turmoil of storm
pounding rain,
thunder might have spoken to him,
telling of what comes and goes
and of what remains.
But the sky hung blank,
the light a powdery oxide,
known elsewhere in its elemental state,
and the lake was sour pewter,
cold and still as ice.

Walking toward him came a woman,
and as they passed,
he met her eyes
already raised to his;
and as they passed
she smiled to him.

He was as if naked,
so maybe now
he couldn't help but
feel the warmth of her
smile. He had nothing else,
and yet who can explain it,
the mystery of being touched?
He said he came back
new to himself,
and from then on
he wanted everyone
to know of the stranger's smile,
how it asked him to agree with his maker,
to be,
to live,
to leave footprints on the earth.

Franklin Gillette

CREATION

Spreading newsprint
on basement cement,
I charcoaled Michelangelo's
Sistine Chapel fresco graph.
I was a teenager,
tracing its hundred scenes.
Un-swept pebbles punctured
paper sprawl,
and I knelt.
Puckered holes, creases, tears,
grew more abundant
than the thoughtful lines
I left unfinished.

        Again, I ruminate,
re-drawing the Book of the Beginning,
re-creating Renaissance recreations—
worlds, galaxies, dimensions,
hopes, evocations, traces left behind,
re-emerging in a contemporary world,
like last night's rain
        now floating under bridges.

Franklin Gillette

ADAM AND EVE

Amidst twisted nudes,
ram skulls, kings,
prophets holding book and scroll,
and civilizations
plagued by falling snakes,
earth's Architect flies in purple robes,
divides earth from water, banishes
the Adversary.
      Serenely with His throngs,
He reaches, touches the primal man,
enlivening…awakening him
to gentle music at the dawn of spring.

Adam feels his limbs
and marvels.

My spirit bathes in opening skies
where atoms explode into galaxies.
The mighty influx of love is constant.
I see nebulas flow like ink in water,
cocoon globules, galactic systems,
astral planes, quasars, phantom planets,
and mysterious trans-dimensional creases.
They move in my blood.
      I feel
human aspirations, insecurities,

fears, joys, empathies, raw desire
move in me out of other beings
move in other beings out of me.

Every mite crawling across rock,
every spore living on continents
of pumpkins and cucumbers, each alien
aloof in every other galaxy,
has made some imprint on my mind.

Underwater, I hold creation's bubble.
Soon, its air will enter my lungs,
as I whisper into silent inner worlds.
My face spans skies of the protozoan.

Love rolls vibrantly,
streams in torrents
pours continuously into the void,
renewing, renewing,
lifting running prana into passageways,
surging,
breaking veils,
lifting me out of sleep
and out of dreams,
lifting my hands
so I, too, can create,
lifting my form
past palisades, river sunsets,
and jungle falls.

At night I discover
contours of a back.
>*"What is this?"*
>*"This is your wife."*
>*Waking soprano yawns.*
>*"Discover paradise in her."*

Merging, we gather in the garden
raspberries and coconuts and seeds,
never recognizing how close,
how precarious
is the giant tree's forbidden knowledge
wizening us to perceive
the terms of a divided universe.

Dr. David James

INTERVIEW WITH GOD

Once Christ was born, I decided to take a hands-off
approach. I was tired of the floods, the killings.
I was tired of getting so damn angry. The stories of my wrath
were cliché, even to me. The quiet path
of least resistance seemed like the smart thing
to try. Instead of being a hard ass, I'd be soft

and forgiving. In the long run, it's been good for my heart,
though I admit, every now and then, I miss
sending down a brutal plague
or the spectacle of a burning bush.
There's a difference, now,
in the way people pray, less push,
less fear. I guess you could call me a purist—
if someone believes, then I'll try to do my part.

Dr. David James

INTERVIEW WITH AN ANGEL

I'm not unhappy. There are perks
to the job—
wings and free air miles,
this cool halo,
the softest bed of clouds you'll ever find.
Of course, it's not all roses.
We're required to turn a blind
eye when people sin, kill,
or rape. We can't throw
our weight around. And God has Her quirks
like anyone else. I've seen Her pissed
beyond words, and it ain't pretty, believe me.
You don't want to be anywhere close
when she's upset—ripping through trees,
hurling lightning bolts,
Her wind pulling out your hair.
But it's a good gig, mostly.
We're filled with divine hope
and can't remember what we miss.

Stephanie Renée dos Santos

THE SAND POET

Mist volplanes over the bay, obscuring the coastal mountaintops. The poet makes her way down the stone staircase, balancing on her cane. She lowers herself onto the rounded rocks, sidesteps patches of seaweed, and then walks out across the sand. Water seeps into her footprints.

She draws her shawl tight across her breast and pulls on the tip of her braid, a woven strand of silver and white. She casts her eyes over the piles of jumbled kelp, scanning for sea treasures brought in from the night tide.

Gulls lift and settle in scattered groups.

She makes her way along the shoreline. Her walking stick trails behind, scratching a warbled path into the wind-blown crust.

Bluffs of sand bulge from the fore dunes, as she skirts their tufted bases. She pauses, as wet gusts blow up the shore.

Gazing out to sea, she watches the waves pile in on top of each other, like seals vying for a space upon a sun-warmed beach.

She sits. Breezes continued to roil.

Words well up and rushed in, sweeping over the topography of her mind, seeking their exit through her hands.

She stands and grasps her stick, and begins to trace words. She organizes them. She cuts each word, each letter into the earth.

Each day gives a new word, a new phrase, or the rearranging of ideas.

She leaves the words there, etched into sand, for all to read: the beach walker, the tourist, the shore birds, the fishermen, the crabs, the children, the winds, and the sea.

These are words left for a short time, before the tides, the rains, the wind, a group of playing children, or an absent-minded adult tromp atop them.

At the poem's end, she thinks, *Yes, that's it*. She accepts its fate—impermanence.

Impermanence cleans her thoughts away, her passions, her miseries, her hopes, her wishes, her word play, away, away, away.

Seated in the sand, next to the last word, she stares out over the sea. She smells the brine and algae, feels her face clammy, and lives the moment, vivid.

The sun burns through the mist. The ocean is lit, with its distant islands of light.

Clouds part, making way for the sun, which descends to be with earth.

Limitless, she thinks. She closes her eyes and tips her head back. *Being*.

She pokes her walking stick into the sand, and helps herself up, onto her crone feet.

She looks up and down the deserted beach, and then to her words.

Let us be as the sea: open and free.

She feels her age in her back and knees, takes hold of the woolen shawl edge, and pulls it over her shoulders.

Another smile peals from her cheeks. She reflects again upon her words, carved into sand.

Her heart beats in time with the waves, the sea carrying her pulse into the expanse. Peace washes through her limbs.

She retraces her footprints.

The words left to the winds, water, and time, and to any passerby.

Tomorrow, she'll be back to leave a sonnet, a phrase, a word, a scratch in the sand, for her pebbled palette will be cleansed.

Craig Evenson

FROM THE PARKING LOT

Sunrise.
The string of water
at the pasture's edge
came out of the darkness,
a fatted marsh
of melted snow.
It returns
with the unrippled interest
of a gracious host—
ecstatic barrel roll,
stretched extremities,
earth-echoed whispers
of commotion calling through
the hollow bones
of the first goose
out of the sky.

Rosemary Dunn Moeller

PERSPECTIVES WITHOUT HORIZONS

Sidewalks are crystal
strewn floors to ants.

The walk up tree trunks
involves sap,
slow molasses creeping
out through breaks in bark,
following a landscape of forms and figures
from another world,
cascading about,
ignoring gravity—
as does the ant
in her slow six-legged ascent to
branches of smoother bark,
pocketed and poxed in shades
of browns and reds,
to the twigs,
to the leaves,
that up so close
as the ant can get,
appear as woven sheets
beaded with sugar crystals
that gleam and glitter,
like a jewelry store case
in the afternoon sunlight.

I envy the ant her tiny world.
Mine's bigger, smoother, rounder,
not so rugged in its
natural beauty, unless
I climb the hills to the peaks of
granite outcroppings, where I
climb along a vertical slate shaft that
once was a seafloor, and
look out at the immensity of the vast plains,
stretching into a dusty infinity
that glimmers as the sun angles down.

John Richmond

AN ALLEGORY FOR OUR TIME

Once upon a time, in a land not so far away and in a kingdom more near than far, there were places called communities. These communities varied in size. Some were very large, while others were very small. Most communities were somewhere in-between.

The people in every community were divided into three groups. There were the Insiders or the Inies; the Outsiders or the Outies; and the Fringe People or the Fringies.

The Inies were people who were from the community. They, for the most part, considered each other to be good.

The Outies were people who were not from the community. They came and went. They were, generally, considered to be up to no good, and even sometimes dangerous.

The Fringies were people who were from the community, but had come to the community within the memory span of the oldest living Inie. At times, the Fringies seemed like Inies, but then they would do something or say something that made the other Inies think that the Fringies really didn't belong.

All communities in the kingdom were mandated to function as smoothly as possible. In order to achieve that goal, the Inies of each community were directed to select one of their own kind to be an Inie Above Inies, to lead them.

On day not so long ago, an Inie Above Inies of a small community sensed that he was no longer as well-liked as he had been, when he was first selected. Indeed, there was even another who wanted to be selected.

The Inie Above Inies—along with his most trusted Keeper, who was in charge of the Keepers of the Community Order—realized that they had only two choices: to do nothing or to do something.

They knew that doing nothing would lead to someone else's being selected. They understood that this would result in their becoming just another of the many Inies.

But the Inie Above Inies had often hoped that he might be selected by the greater kingdom as a King Among Kings. He knew that he must do something.

He could not do something directly, because all of the other Inies would then know that he was weak. Thus, it was decided that the small community must have a distraction.

This could not be just any distraction, however. It could not be a simple, local distraction. It had to be a distraction that would make everyone, far and wide throughout the kingdom, pay attention to this particular Inie Above Inies.

The Inie Above Inies and the Keeper decided that, by distracting the community in a way that seemed as if it were no design of their own, they could raise the Inie Above Inies to the proportions of a Near-To-Living-God-Among-Us, who would challenge, confront, and defeat the distraction. So, no one else would be selected, and the Inie Above Inies might go on to become a King Among Kings.

But the Inie Above Inies was puzzled. What could the distraction be? It couldn't be an ordinary distraction, like festival water that was too warm or flap-flight food that was too cold. No, not everyone drinks festival water or even cares whether the flap-flight food is cold, so long as the water and the food are there, in front of them. These would not be good distractions.

The Inie Above Inies and the Keeper realized that the best distraction would be one that affected everyone.

But what could it be?

The air? The sun? The darkness?

Of course, the darkness! Yes, the greatest distraction would be a period of darkness that does not relent to the light of day. That way, the Inie Above Inies could step forward and command the darkness away.

They knew that this was the greatest of all distractions, because everyone in the community was afraid of too much darkness. When darkness fell, strange things could happen, things that the Inies did not understand.

But neither the Inie Above Inies nor the Keeper could figure out a way to create the darkness, much less to make the darkness go away.

Yes, darkness was a good distraction, but this distraction had to be a different kind of darkness.

The Inie Above Inies and the Keeper began to think about all that the other Inies did not understand. They understood each other, because Inies understand all other Inies. What the Inies did not and would never understand, however, were the Outies.

"Yes, of course, the Outies," they reasoned. The community has always had problems with Outies.

The Inies knew that the Outies would, if given the chance, steal their property, defile their women, emasculate their men, and take away everything that the Inies had worked for. It was a great idea.

There was, however, only one problem.

"We have so few Outies," the Inie Above Inies lamented. "We know who they are, and we know when they come into the community."

No, the Outies were not suitable. The distraction needed to be closer to the community.

The Keeper nodded. With the Inie Above Inies, he retired to the sanctuary to think deeply. There, in their most private and sacred of places, they thought and they thought, but to no avail.

Finally, the Keeper suggested that they bathe in the most holy of festival water, so that they might be inspired. Perhaps they had not given proper deference and homage to the god that had inspired countless generations of their ancestors.

Hours of prayerful vigilance passed. Then, the Keeper arose from the deepest level of prayerful reverie. He simply said, "Fringies."

"Fringies?" asked the Inie Above Inies.

"Yes, the Fringies."

The Keeper spoke about how the Fringies really hated all of the Inies. Why else would they continue to talk strange, dress strange, act strange, and be strange? Yes, they were living among the Inies now, but they were really aligned with the Outies.

The Keeper asked the Inie Above Inies what he thought about his idea.

"I'm not sure that they want to steal and defile and emasculate," the Inie Above Inies said.

"It doesn't matter," he was told. "Whether they want to or not doesn't matter. All we have to do is make it seem like they do, and you will be re-selected."

"But how can this be done?" the Inie Above Inies asked.

"Leave it to me," was the answer from the Keeper.

In due time, the Keeper found a Fringie who was failing the community for his own gain. It was discovered that this Fringie named Fringad, who was appointed to guard the festival water, was helping himself to portions of it.

The Keeper confronted Fringad and told him that either he had to help with the Inie Above Inie's re-selection, or that he, Fringad, would be banished from the community.

Fringad considered himself to be as good as any Inie, but still, he knew that he was different. Reluctantly, he agreed to help.

The Keeper told Fringad that he must make it seem that some of the Fringies were helping the Outies in their attempt to destroy the community.

Fringad hesitated, but the Keeper told him that he would be given extra bread for his effort.

On his way out of the meeting, the Keeper reminded Fringad that he would be watched and followed by the Keepers of the Community Order.

Soon, Fringad was able to convince a number of other Fringies to help him. They made it appear as if the Outies were attacking the community. They felled trees over the main roads going into and out of the community. They floated logs in the pond where the community drew its water, and they built fires in the hills that overlooked the community.

Upon each occurrence, the Inies were frightened.

After each occurrence, the Inie Above Inies arrived with the Keeper and the Keepers of the Community Order to show the community that they had nothing to fear. The community found new respect for the Inie Above Inies. They forgot about selecting anyone else.

But Fringad was unhappy.

Over time, he came not to care about the extra bread.

"This is not enough," he shouted. "I want festival water, but the Keeper denies me."

Soon, he began to think of getting back at the Keeper. He wanted revenge. His Fringie accomplices, too, began to sympathize with Fringad.

"They only give us the old bread," one Fringie shouted.

"We want the same bread as they eat," said another.

Fringad smiled and understood what they must do.

"Tonight, we will trample their grain fields!" he announced.

That night, as they were trampling the grain in a field, they encountered a number of Outies.

The Outies were curious as to why these Fringies were turning on their own kind.

"We are angry," one Fringie said.

"We want to get back at them," said another.

The Outies needed to hear no more. They began to instruct the Fringies on how to make life fearful for the Inies.

Meanwhile, the Inie Above Inies was getting closer and closer to being re-selected. When he heard that the fields of grain had been trampled and two cows killed, however, he called on the Keeper.

"This is not suppose to be real," the Inie Above Inies, said. "You must put a stop to it."

The Keeper gave the Inie Above Inies his word that it would stop.

The Keeper was a dedicated defender of the community. He began to watch, follow, and track Fringad. He used the Keepers of the Community Order to pursue and capture the troublemaking Fringies.

After a time, only Fringad was left. He was an elusive quarry, keen and hard to capture.

The Keeper knew that Fringad could no longer be trusted. Rumors that Fringad had sworn to destroy the community began to circulate.

The Keeper knew that if Fringad were to stay true to his oath, then he would have to destroy the sanctuary. Further, the Keeper understood that if Fringad could destroy the sanctuary, then no place would be safe.

So, the Keeper stopped trying to follow Fringad. Instead, the Keeper went to the Inie Above Inies and told him about what he believed Fringad's plans to be.

Late that evening, the Inie Above Inies and the Keeper hid within the sanctuary. They sat quietly. They waited patiently.

Finally, Fringad appeared. In his right hand, he held a torch, and in his left, a sack of dirt.

The Inie Above Inies and the Keeper knew that Fringad was not only going to burn down the sanctuary. He was going to taint the festival water, too.

With due haste, the Keeper stepped from the shadows and confronted Fringad.

"Stop. What do you think you are doing?" the Keeper called out.

Fringad stated his intentions and drew a knife. "No one is going to stop me now," he said.

The Keeper drew his own knife.

They fought, but Fringad was no match for the Keeper.

Once Fringad had fallen, the Inie Above Inies stepped from the shadows. "Has he gone?" the Inie Above Inies asked.

"Yes," the Keeper replied.

"Then we are finally finished with this matter," said the Inie Above Inies.

"Almost, but not yet," said the Keeper.

"What is left?" asked the Inie Above Inies.

The Keeper, reached down, picked up Fringad's knife, and slashed the Inie Above Inies across the arm.

"What are you doing?" shouted the Inie Above Inies.

The Keeper returned the knife to Fringad's dead hand and put his own knife into the hand of the Inie Above Inies. Then, he began shouting. "Inies, Inies, come out and see. The one you selected has saved the sanctuary. He has stopped one who would have destroyed it. Inies, come out and see one who is great."

Annette Barnes

Topics for a Book Club Discussion

Recommended for ages six and above.

1. Sing a Song of Six Pence

Is it right to bake blackbirds?
Do kings deserve a dish daintier
than cottage pie, or shepherd's pie?

Consider whether being English
influences your answers. Would
a Chinese or an African answer in
the same way? Would a Scot?

2. Little Miss Muffet

A tuffet is…
a. a clump of grass
b. a small hillock
c. a foot stool
d. a pillow
e. all of the above
f. none of the above

Should the spider have asked permission
to sit next to Miss Muffet?

Consider whether spiders can be held
to the same standard as humans.

3. Old King Cole

King Cole was...
a. magnificent
b. old
c. a saint
d. planning to play the flute
f. about to eat some soup
g. inconsiderate to call for things so late at night

Were any of the fiddlers women? Discuss whether
their presence or absence should be of concern.

4. Humpty Dumpty

Humpty Dumpty was...
a. a king
b. a cannon
c. an egg

Did Humpty Dumpty merit the attention
of so many of the king's men?

Discuss how one should allocate emergency
relief resources.

David Alan Goldstein

MOTHER LOVE

I had always believed that I became who I was in spite of my mother, not because of her. It was not until I was fifty-six years old that I understood my mother had been a good one.

Through twenty years of married life and two wives, I found plenty of support for the notion that my mother had been a bad one. For a time, I believed that two failed marriages proved that my mother had "done it wrong."

After my third marriage, however, I began to understand my mother and our relationship quite differently.

When I married for the third time, I found the mothering I had never had, a kind of mothering I believed was somehow better than what I had been given. Old wounds healed, and I began to appreciate my mother for who she was.

A man cannot apologize to a gravestone, though that is what I did. I am still uncertain as to whether or not I felt any better for that act.

* * *

The long silence between my mother and me began after the marriage to my second wife, Lisa.

Before marrying, I flew with Lisa to Florida, so that she could meet my mother.

My mother was a vacant shell, shuffling about in a house dress, and saying nothing. She and Lisa had exchanged barbs on the phone, even before meeting.

"We have to invite her to the wedding," I said to Lisa, when we returned.

"She'll make us miserable."

"Probably so," I said. "You'll survive."

"Great," Lisa said, but she made the phone call.

"Oregon is just so far away," my mother said.

"It is. . .I know," Lisa said with apparent agreement, while frowning at me. "But we'd really like you to come to the wedding," she added.

"I just don't know," mother said. "It rains a lot in Oregon, doesn't it?"

"People get used to it," Lisa replied without thinking.

"People get used to all kinds of things."

Lisa began to fumble. The words came out in bits and pieces.

"He's. . .your son. . .He's your. . .only son."

"Well, I don't know. I could buy a raincoat. I'll think about it. But what use do I have for a raincoat, here in Miami. I don't know. I'll think about it."

Lisa waited, silent.

"What month did you say?"

"October."

"Rainy season. Say 'hi' to Martin."

Lisa hung up. The first words she said were, "What a difficult woman."

I nodded in agreement. "She certainly never made life easy," I said.

Really, she had made life easy. I just didn't realize it, at the time. She had paid for an Ivy League education, graduate school, and my first car. She had loaned me money for a down payment on a house. Later, she forgave the debt.

Still, Lisa and my mother would never be friends. This was a fact of who they were.

My mother's past was something not spoken about. All that I knew, I knew through the words of an aunt.

Both of my mother's parents had died by the time she was four. My mother had no memory of her father. She had a single memory of her mother's waving to her from the window of a hospital room, she a child in a white dress standing on a lawn somewhere looking up at a window, perhaps only thinking that she was seeing the hand of her mother waving.

Lisa, though, knew her mother too well. Lisa's mother had beaten her so often and so brutally that the very word "mother" could mean only one thing—pain.

Every verbal barb from my mother raised welts upon my wife. And so it was that Lisa would say, "I'm so sorry you have the mother you do."

There were times when I said the same thing to Lisa. "I'm so sorry you had the mother you did."

From this we forged our common bond.

My mother did attend our wedding. She carried no umbrella but arrived with a suitcase of verbal barbs that fell like a whip upon my wife.

The truth is that my mother was as afraid of Lisa as Lisa was of my mother. Each saw her own past in the other. They were two discarded children, motherless, raised by strangers. They were both lone survivors in a frightening world.

After the wedding, my wife and my mother did not speak to each other again. Each dutifully sent the other birthday and Christmas gifts, with the cards signed simply, "Love, Lisa" or "Love, Mom."

I did not see my mother for the length of my marriage to Lisa. I spoke to her regularly but with a new distance. I had been forced to choose.

Towards the end of my marriage to Lisa, during our separation, my mother almost died.

She was then seventy-eight years old. She was losing two things: memory and physical balance.

Her solution? She swallowed all the prescription medicine in the medicine chest.

Her effort failed. Although her body survived, however, her spirit vanished.

I visited her several months after she was released from the hospital. Her skin had gone ashy gray. She barely spoke and seldom left her home.

During the five years before she died, I visited her regularly. I made the long trip from Oregon, first as a divorced middle-aged man, and then with a new wife, Angel.

My mother approved of my marriage to Angel. All barbs were gone from her, now. She resisted nothing, except perhaps death. She was a changed woman.

I found new satisfaction in her mothering. I was pleased that she believed I had found my life mate, that she saw Angel as a good and caring woman. Somehow, she saw me as a good man, too.

I began to appreciate all that my mother had given me. She had offered her best, if flawed, effort. She had forgiven me my debt and even taught me self-reliance.

These last years of my mother's life became the happiest of mine.

* * *

Only long after events have played out can we look back and understand them. Had I appreciated all that my mother had given me, would I have spent so many years without seeing her? And years from now, will I understand things in a still different way?

I do not believe that wisdom comes with aging. Rather, I believe that wisdom comes with time. We act in the present and understand in the future.

No matter our age, our present actions are inevitably ignorant. We may think before we act, but always we act without perspective.

Perspective arises only when consequences are known.

It is then too late to alter the act. We are left satisfied, if at all, only because we understand.

Lyn Lifshin

ASPARAGUS

When I see the early green, I'm flung
back to that spring: the news of the
tumor, the words "inoperable" and "palliative,"
like guns. Asparagus was in the stores, even as
snow still fell in Stowe, in May. The darkness
hung in. Asparagus was almost the only thing
my mother would still eat, cooked to be
soft, salted, buttered. This was before
the IV drip made her ankles swell. My sister
took the salt away, though she had once said it was
stupid to take chocolate from an old man
in a rest home, so that he wouldn't ruin his
teeth. My mother wanted pale jade clothes,
as if she could feel green going out
of her life. "I just love the green," she said.
For the past few summers she'd disliked tiger
lily orange. "It's the color of fall," she'd moan.
"It means that summer is over."
All spring I ate asparagus with her,
picking out the thinnest stalks. In two
more months, she would have been 80.
In a Vermont restaurant
I've rarely been to since
my 16th birthday party,
I order salmon.
It's puzzling to me to read in notes

that salmon was what
my mother ordered there
on her last New Year's Eve,
even though she couldn't swallow it.
I'm wearing her socks
and her ring. I find myself
with saltine crackers,
bran waffles, asparagus, and strawberries.
It's as if the bits of her I carry inside me—
as one writer said, "We do our mothers,
like dolls, each with another inside"—
are with me in the supermarkets, where she
could spend hours filling my cart, as she
did my life, with what she
wanted for me

Lyn Lifshin

WINTERGREEN

It was always in my mother's pocket book—
wintergreen wedged between eye glasses, a broken
watch, coupons, lipsticks, and the keys she was
sure she'd lost. In her last days, she
insisted that the Lifesavers be on the night-stand
near the bed, there to keep her from coughing
or throwing up pills. Like Joy perfume and
Jolie Madame, a whiff of wintergreen is
the smell of my mother. Wintergreen was
the color she always chose
in her last years, as she longed
for emeralds, as she longed
for green to clear through late
Vermont winter snow. She seemed already
lost and scared. She was terrified if
she called, and I didn't pick up the phone.
When I see a field of wintergreen,
when I smell the mint,
I want to scoop it up and bring it to her.
Peppermint or spearmint wouldn't do. It was
wintergreen in silver foil, clean and fresh as
a night when stars are silver fish, the moon a
silver apple. I wonder why I didn't make a tea
of it for her. I wonder if anything else growing smells
as fresh. When we drove in Murray's car
past Silver Moon Diner, thru Cranberry Bogs

my mother asked if I'd like a mint, gave me
the wintergreen roll, smelling of her
lilac-scented lipstick and Marlboros and
Tareytons, the sweetness melting as the city
did behind us, the sweetness comforting
as air on the first day of snow,
when nothing is stained or walked on.

Lyn Lifshin

MY MOTHER AND THE ORANGES

Under the afghan
on velvet squares,
my mother dozed
among orange peels.
"I love," she says, "to
fall asleep with
the lights on and
someone talking." I
think of the paint-
ing of her as a
child in a peach
chiffon dress, clutching
her little brother, her
eyes enormous, locked
inside a silver frame.
The year I was six,
I woke up each night
by midnight howl-
ing, was cuddled
in her huge blue
bed in the room
over the falls,
where I'd get into
bed with hot cocoa
on Friday nights
for radio programs

I remember less
clearly than the
blue wool blankets.
The oranges I peel
make her smack her
lips before she
tastes them, want-
ing the orange
slivers nestled like
little babies, deep
and close between
the bigger slices,
like something
held close in dark-
ness, before the
skin's pulled a-
way and what has
been held
tightly together
begins to split.

Lyn Lifshin

THAT LAST AFTERNOON MY MOTHER WANTS BREAD AND BUTTER IN MILK

It's as if she is already
stepping back, moving
into a place she can't
take me to with her. She
doesn't want my fingers
on her skin. It's the
first time she doesn't
want her back rubbed,
or touched. I am moving
back to the green
carpet, ripped and
faded, past the
stained glass in the
hall and up to where
wasps once fell on their
backs. My mother
doesn't eat the bread
she wanted. I sit on the
grass this morning,
see the leaves dying.
My mother almost tasted
the bread and butter her
mother would bring
out to her on the porch, as
roses sucked on the

mango and amber
light before dark.

Carl Alessi

A WORD TO THE WISE GUY

The sky has eyes,
but the trees have no ears.
And death?
He lives in a little basement pad
over on Eight Street.
He passes his days
reading old pulp books from the Thirties.
Death knows he's got all the time in the world.
He has centuries,
maybe even aeons ahead of him.
It looks like he has it made,
and why not?
Isn't that the way the boss
arranged everything
a long, long time ago?

J. J. Deur

ALICIA'S UNLUCKY DAY

Alicia came out to meet police. It was the only natural thing to do. When you call the police, you meet the police. Alicia's complaint was about a stolen truck—Alicia's stolen truck, that is. But it wasn't Alicia's lucky day.

When you deal with police, it is never your lucky day. Logic tells you that.

If you expect the events to turn out otherwise, you admit that you are a full of it—even as an unintended big fool, a self-made big fool.

Police would agree with you on that one every time, should you ask them about it. They share a common logic with you, as long as you are on the losing end.

In this case, the police had another Alicia on their mind—Alicia Tucker.

You told them that you were Alicia Dexter, but they didn't believe you.

You showed them your driver's license, and they still didn't believe you.

You showed your deed on the house from which you had called them, about your stolen truck. They still didn't believe you.

You asked them, "If you don't believe that I am Alicia Dexter, then which Alicia am I?"

They told you, "You are the poor and guilty Alicia."

You temporarily ignored the word "poor" and focused on the word "guilty."

You asked them, "Guilty of what?" (And then you told them that you have a house and that you are not poor, just for the sake of it.)

They responded, "Guilty of aggravated assault."

You told them that it must be a different Alicia, because your birth date doesn't match, your address doesn't match, and your description doesn't match. You emphasized that only the name Alicia matches, but that nothing else matches.

The police told you that the judge would answer that question for them.

They offered you a seat in their police car, and you ended up there, under the arrest warrant, on the way to meet the judge. You thought that you were dreaming, but you were afraid to ask police to pinch you to verify it, the old-fashioned way.

The tricky judge believed the police and not you—the Alicia who had called police about your stolen truck. And you, the same Alicia, were going to spend 53 days in jail on the judge's referral.

After spending time in jail, now you are an Alicia 53 days older. You are a different Alicia, even to yourself. You are the Alicia without the truck and with the new title, "ex-convict."

One might say, "You are now angry-beyond-yourself Alicia."

You walk in an ever-present mental daze. When you sense a police car on the avenue, your radar antenna pulls you into a side street. You fear everything that runs on a gas-guzzling motor, anything that reminds you of the police car.

Next time, should someone ask you for your identity papers, you'll offer them a chance to take a blueprint of your eyes. Your past experience will be a watchdog for your future.

So, you, Alicia, lost your truck, and 53 days of your precious life, while you were an honorary guest in the slammer, just because you called police about your stolen truck on the unluckiest day of your life.

The rest was in your lawyer's hands—the one that you are still shopping around for.

Barry W. North

AUGUST IS NOT AUGUST

It never has been
and, I'm tempted to say,
never will be,
but in today's fragile world,
nothing except our
unbreakable resolve
to trash the planet
can be relied upon
to remain constant.
I would not be surprised
to wake up one morning and learn
that our unbridled pollution
had finally reached into the heavens
and was beginning to darken the stars,
and was starting to shuffle
the seasons around down here
like cards in a deck,
causing even always predictable August
to abruptly,
and without any warning—
like a dying patient
sitting bolt upright in bed—
shed its dog day persona,
take on the mantle of majestic December,
and spread a blanket of snow
across the Northeast

and even down into the deep South,
putting the fear of God
into anybody who has ever
cursed or prayed
for the end.

Leslie Plajzer

SOBRIETY

I couldn't find a job.

I didn't have skills for what would have been an "acceptable job," but I was too pompous for anything else. My resume showed employment gaps. I interviewed poorly.

I had been sober for about three months. I didn't want to admit that I was just as unemployable as the next drunk.

Still, my money had run out. I had food stamps and was waiting for my first welfare check.

Then, I was hired by a store that sold character telephones in a local mall.

Any gratitude I felt was overshadowed by remorse and the phony air of self-importance I used to get by. I had no God, so I covered my insecurities with arrogance. I masked shame with an attitude that reeked of entitlement.

Really, I was the antithesis of what I portrayed. I was a timid little girl who, at thirty years of age, didn't want to be a drunk. Being an unemployable drunk was that much worse.

I had never touched a cash register, pushed a broom, or seen the inside of a stock room, so I behaved like the consummate victim.

I was consumed with self-pity and envy. I found no joy in getting sober.

Waiting on customers felt like subservience. My actions were right on, but my affect was like that of an angry adolescent. I was jealous of children whose mothers who were in the store buying Christmas presents for them.

Mickey Mouse phones became a subversive tool to make me feel inferior.

I walked around the mall during breaks to let off steam. My feelings were tough to mask. My preoccupation with a shot of whiskey was growing.

Still, I thought Sir Lancelot was waiting in the parking lot to rescue me.

I shunned conversation with other employees. I moved as though I had a destination, refusing to engage, interact, or make eye contact with anyone.

Anyone that is, except Aubrey.

Aubrey was the janitor. A gentleman in his seventies he was tall and lean, with a cheerful demeanor. If he wasn't on a ladder, he was pushing a mop or pulling a pail of soapy water. He swept trash, waxed floors, cleaned bathrooms, and chatted with my boss over coffee each morning.

He was gracious enough to evoke a sociable response— even from me.

If Aubrey smiled, I smiled back. If Aubrey spoke, I spoke back. If Aubrey asked where I was headed, I told him I was going nowhere.

Between Thanksgiving and Christmas my spirit grew depleted. I was lonelier than I had ever thought possible.

I could no longer pretend that this was a bad dream. I was not royalty. The walkways in the mall were not tree-lined streets leading to Buckingham Palace. Prince Charming was not waiting for me between the large department stores at either end of the complex.

I was a retail sales clerk whose life was ending on a sour note. Angry consumers were yelling at me, because I was distant, inattentive, and lost in a world of my own. I refused to memorize the product line. I couldn't focus long enough to make a return. I always missed a dust bunny, when I swept at night.

I was preoccupied with drinking, paralyzed in a pity party of negativity. I found myself living out the Alcoholics Anonymous slogan, "Poor me, poor me, pour me a drink."

I shared in meetings about wanting to drink but refused suggestions from acquaintances in recovery.

"Find a meeting during the day" I was told. "Work late, go in early, take a long lunch, and find a meeting close to the mall where you work."

Finally, the yearning for what was familiar became all-consuming. I was ready to head for the liquor store.

I did stop to pick up the telephone.

Slowly, I dialed the number.

"My name is Leslie W.," I told the gentleman manning the Alcoholics Anonymous hotline. "I've been sober for five months, but I'm going to drink if I don't get to a meeting. I'm working at a store in the Columbia Mall. I don't know how to get to a meeting." I started to cry. "I need help. I don't want to drink. Can you tell me how to get to a meeting from the Columbia Mall?"

"I'm coming to get you, right now," the man said.

Ten minutes later, he arrived at the mall and was by my side. It was Aubrey.

Aubrey didn't answer my prayers, but he gave me permission to pray. He wasn't the path I embarked on, but he was the point where I got on the road. He didn't complete the puzzle, but he gave me the ability to pause without forcing the pieces.

What I remember most about my first sober job isn't the fantasies I used to cover my fear and envy. It wasn't about the food stamps I got or the welfare check I had to return. It wasn't about the shot of whiskey I wanted, the Mickey Mouse phones I still find on eBay some twenty-five years later, the marketable skills I didn't have, or the exaggerated tale of self-importance I wove to comfort my half-beaten soul. It was about an unexpected happening, an offering that the universe made. It was about the day I accepted a world of possibilities.

I remember that phone call as the moment I rethought the way life works. The dots on the canvas—are they really random?

Rebecca Lilly

HAIKU

i.

The clouds sweep off; hills,
valleys, tinged with green; a wind
follows the wooded stream

Spontaneous and
effortless, how thought should be:
here, then dissolving. . .

ii.

Like a hollowed-out
mossed log, the wind's raw throat; rain
spots the rotted bark

Observe yourself in
joy and sadness both; learn to
act on the balance

Dr. Edward Bruce Bynum

CONSCIOUSNESS RETURNING

There is a consciousness returning,
a rain-fed and furious consciousness,
a consciousness of iron and history
and beautiful omens
making its way back to this earth
in the living river of fate and blood.
I see it from the hills, where the night thickens.
The moon commands,
when the cyclical hour of eternity touches down
on these terrestrial shores.
The hour of the maggot and the war-dog
are crumbling. The blue hemisphere of the child
rises from the bog. The market pit
and the bestial flower
wake the army of snake-men
from their slithering graves.
Solitude is shaken
from rocks and alluvial places,
brought to the fire,
dumped into the coals, where it foments
into islands. The new spirit has
taken into air like a burning comet
passing a primal lightning through our bones.
Out of the woods,
out of the winding alleyway of the cities,
out of the mute eyes,

out of the hollow bellies of the poor,
from the guttural music of the pious,
of the faithful
and the distracted,
across vast intemperate seas
comes this new wave of incandescent thunder.
The wise and beautiful
have waited lifetime
after lifetime to see
what brings the bright noise
of our adolescent hours
to an end.
Above, the hammers and octaves of insight,
the round chorus of birds, and the trees
we wake to in the morning
will bend, twist, and unlock their ears.
Sunlight, making no mistakes,
will sever the darkness.
With a wave of summer,
the mint from a million gardens
will deepen tea and opulent wines.
We are citizens of the world yet to be.
There is a consciousness returning
in a sidereal spiral,
in a music of flutes.
It awakens
the thin luminous strings in the spine,
the opaque snake
of our higher science.
It sleeps deep in the dark coil

and still forbidden coccyx of the mind.
There will be no need for memory.
Everything is happening at once.
Nails and garbage will evaporate.
The sound of pistols will be banished like mold.
Weather is one long geography
of innocence and potential.
Whatever remains of acid
and the dispatched coal of locomotives
will instruct us in ways that
time is still preparing to bring us,
on the ragged waves of the future.
There is a consciousness returning.
It has the ambition of waters
to break down, to clean
things, to wash away limits ascribed
to barriers and religions.
Its tools mimic the revolutions of the hand,
and the small sordid rumors spreading
like pestilential winds through the night.
Open your mouth, and receive it.
Open your heart and your wide variable soul.
Release your breath into its contagious presence.
Drop your enemies into it,
like the dead baby bundle
cast into the Ganges or Nile,
swept down the river,
becoming the food of crocodiles
that lunge up
in the cycle of hope and renewal,

amidst incarnations of grieving parents and loss.
There is no rational way to enjoy this.
There is no theory of beauty or balance
or animal flower moving in us
to explain the rare oil and music
that comes out of this.
In death there are oblivious strangers
who walk through each other.
But we know this.
In dreams there are passageways of characters,
lurid caves full of dancers,
rows of spice and books lined with incantations.
But we know this.
There are poems already written,
waiting for poets
to awaken them.
But we know this.
My soul has returned from the age of stone and stars,
from the age of initiations and rivers.
It is crossing again with my brothers and sisters
the distances over matter and death,
touching again the beginning of beginnings.
In the body there are highways,
fortresses, and encampments,
where blood hides and prepares to battle
again and again.
The enemy pulls us like gravity,
like distant bells,
like creatures born of nightwalks and lobotomies
back to the black island,

the reef of doubt,
the isle of the shipwrecked,
the beach of flies. My body
is your body. My tongue
is your tongue.
Feel the bloodlines in my hands.
We share the same orbit,
the same heartbeat,
the same unearthly swallow
flying with its luminous tail
from life to life.
We exchange bodies,
like the ocean exchanges waters
from the cycle of rivers
that empty themselves
full of vibrancy, leaves, and teeth.
Into the long blue estuary of hours, we are born.
There is a consciousness returning.

Joseph Dorazio

GOLD ANKLEBONE CUPS
After Sappho

They sought the truth
and were venerated, but
all that remains are a few
bits and pieces: skull bowls,
gold anklebone cups,
Buddha's tooth.

Paul Hansom

The Passing Place

i.

We wound into Inverpolly National Reserve on the single lane road, across a flat plain, past Stac Pollaidh that juts up like Dracula's castle, its ragged back ending in the infamous Lobster Claw.

Once up there with Sue, I'd gone on alone. Having reached the crumbling edge, I stood gazing at the absolute limit of the British Isles. Miles away, the white caps were crashing onto the cliffs. The Atlantic stretched itself into nothing—and then fog, sudden and soundless.

I couldn't see a foot in front of me. I was tapping with my stick, knowing I could blunder off at any point.

I heard someone shouting. Maybe, Sue was calling my name, but I didn't answer. Yelling in the fog like that seemed a bit daft, with the rocks suddenly new, with silence in physical form, with each droplet of water hanging perfect in the air.

I didn't want to be found.

We passed a lot of little tarns, neither pond nor lake, filled with black bog water, a tin hut at the edge, a rowing boat waiting patiently for the fisherman who'd never come again.

I wondered briefly what it would be like, sitting out there. I wondered whether there'd be some new perspective, some distinct vantage point.

Somehow, I knew it would be the same as every other angle, the same treeless vista, the same lichen-mottled stones, that it would be emptiness unpeopled, without relics, but for the occasional German in his growling campervan.

We'd come from Ullapool, where I ate ice cream, sat on the sea wall, and watched the trawlers.

The sea stinks. The seals break water for air, like so many bowling balls.

The trawlers rarely go out. There's nothing to fish and little money for fuel. The boats are a bit of a hobby. They are an old habit dying very hard.

This town's like all the rest. Ugly. It is the dead end of history with its old lady trundling down to the shop for her beans and cat food, as she wonders briefly about her wee hubby in his weathered grave.

You hope that there may be something special in the cemetery, that there might be some grand testament to heroic fishers or sailors, but this is like any other Scottish cemetery. It is stuffed with hundred-year-old Victorian platitudes. The dead sleep forever, their bones rat-nipped and green.

Ullapool is the biggest town in the region and dull as anything. The knickknack shops sell wool and Chinese brass to tourists. Standing between the chip shop and the butcher's place, you wonder what's really Scottish. Clearly it's not the pricey whiskey or the loch-farmed salmon. It's not the heaving pub, bursting with bored backpackers who are jostling elbows with the quaymen boozing at noon.

For an Englander in the Highlands, there's always that thrilling pause when you open your mouth, that split-second tribal flicker, when they recognize you as the ancient enemy.

And there's decay, of course. That's authentic enough. Those dead crofts cleared off long ago. The villagers fled to Canada for a new life, because this one was obviously kicked.

I've seen the old photographs in the empty Heritage Center of the subsistence farming and the filthy wool-dyeing. You see clearly that any life here was hard, lousy, and violent, that it's a past not worth celebrating.

But the rock ruins are still here, scattered in the dips, gullies, and human trash.

I have wished for a ghost, but none would be caught dead around here.

This is a place at the end of things. The screaming drunk beats his faithful dog and raves about the IRA. What is he but some soldier, some phantom hung up for retirement, an ex-copper stashed away from all those he's sent down?

Here is pure dereliction.

Pull in for petrol, and there's nobody in the office, nobody to pay or pump. Stumble onto some artisan junk, a gallery culture alive here with its overpriced oils, watercolors, hippy pots, and plates. Turn anywhere and find a thriving colony in a converted D-Day army base, thick with that desperate air of people far away from the center of things. They kid themselves that they're being true to a vision. You see it in those dead eyes, those tired faces. The weaver is making it with the potter; the potter is slightly in love with the candlestick maker, who's just quit the engraver.

They are bored unto death with the gray seagulls sailing endless rain. They hate tourists with the only passion left unto them. They make you pay for that.

All places are crap, if you look hard enough. They're crap, if you choose the wrong path.

But sometimes, the crap is sublime. Sometimes, it's got real power.

I have been moved here. I have seen poetry in a dead sprat lying on the dry sand shoal. Its marble eye reflects my face, as the clouds scud around my hat.

Out on those rocks that slip to the sea, like colossal sinking decks, I've clambered for miles in the sun, without a trace of fatigue.

I know a boy should be on the rocks. It's the only place for him, really. The fringes. Here, he feels vast and empty. He is cultivating defiance. He is shaping his courage. Still, solitude tips towards loneliness, and then sadness.

Later in life, I feel the ebb. The body's willing but the mind won't shut up. *Don't go too far. Don't risk much. Recognize the point of return, so you can get back home.*

Down the road, past Achiltibuie, Badenscallie, and Achduart to Culnacraig, the cottage sits on its hillside. Behind it, the black mountain hunches. This may be the last time I'll ever be here, because my parents are old. They're the next dead on the list. They can't manage the drive, carting up their taties, the beer, the *boule*, and those hopeful summer togs.

ii.

The place hasn't changed much. There is a new kettle, a new washer, and new satellite TV. These are things to keep the bored holiday-makers happy.

But the guts are the same—the charming tat, that copper bed-warmer, ancient candlesticks propped beside a bread board. Up the stairs are the plaster busts of child Meg and her brother, and the old pub door to the loo with its racy cartoon.

I've slept in all these rooms, their beds one person wide, hugging like a coffin, high up on their rough-cut cement blocks.

There is nothing to look at, until you're in these beds. Then you see, down across the meadow, out to the endless gray waves. This is some view.

The rooms are still musty and filled with dead spring spiders, their silky pods behind every jumble-sale scoop. This volume tells of a driving tour through Britain, the pages filled with long-gone museums, baths and foundations. An old kid's book tells about the weather. Its pictures hark back to the postwar world, when rain and clouds were special. Morning fog cloaks an English village. A Royal Mail van crawls up the hill. The church steeple flaunts a limp St. George's flag. Later, the fog lifts. There's a Tudor pub, with a Morris parked on the gravel. A suited man and head-squared woman pop in for a pint. Brilliant that.

But the coldest room is downstairs. The bare granite walls offer no insulation. There is nothing between you and the elements. This chamber is more dungeon than bedroom. It's a cave for storing spuds. There will be no sleeping here, thank you. Those surplus cots groan on their last-leg nuts.

Only we've all slept here. Aunty Doris, Uncle Bob, Mum, and Dad, have all taken their turns, complained, and laughed about it, this bit of Scottish lore.

A picture of Meg's brother, circa 1941, watches over all. He was a matinee idol, like they all were back then. In his

RAF uniform, he looks bored, his eyes glassy with a whisky hangover. He is on leave, before flying off for the last time, thinking that this place will always be waiting.

Pictures mirror photographs. Photos hail the paintings, all done by the man in the tintype hanging next to his study of feathers. That's the father. There's a small collage of him, done seventy years ago. He's dressed in plus-fours and tweeds, a fishing creel on one hip, a big salmon in hand.

Large doors lead to rooms and to other doors, in an endless procession of light-filled space. A round table with hydrangeas stands in the sun. A pretty watercolor hangs in the loo. That oak couch with the barley-twist legs is still squeezed into the conservatory. Here are endless echoes.

iii.

Meg Balfour was in her 70s, when we first rented this place. An eccentric English spinster, she lucked into this croft by an act of sheer kindness.

She'd taken care of some old Scottish git, bringing him soups and the like. When his son refused to live in the place after his death, the git willed it to Meg.

Cut the son out. Cut us all in.

Meg was one for the welcomes. She came galumphing across the pasture in her green wellies and man's shirt, with a jaunty bandana fluttering around her throat. This costume was extraordinary for one so old, but people get away with that up here.

"Well, hello!" She always gave the same greeting in that plummy voice, as if we were dropping in for a whisky or a wine.

She was off her trolley, driving her battered Subaru like a nutter. She'd flipped herself into the ditch once or twice, to await the help of the postman on his last rounds. "What larks," she'd thought, without a care.

As a young woman, she'd worked military intelligence in North Africa, knocking around Cairo and Alexandria. These days had all been very dull, according to her. The most notable turn of events had been a nasty sunburn she'd gotten from snoozing in a valley.

The war had brought the love of her life. It had also taken him away. By her own telling, she'd never forgotten him. Although she had endured such strength of loss, she appeared not the least bit maudlin.

"That's just the way it was," she explained crisply.

Meg was from that inner sanctum, the establishment. She had grown up in the lap of luxury. Her childhood days had been filled with private schools and culture. She had even attended a party where Yehudi Menuhin, a kid at the time, had nabbed the last piece of chocolate cake.

She'd known them all—the famous pols, the top ranking civil servants, and Britain's notorious spies.

Sitting in her presence, knee to knee in the cramped conservatory, was extraordinary. Thoughtful, opinionated, oblivious, she had a certainty by which the ruling class rules. I began to understand how lesser people, myself included, could follow a woman like that to the death.

I didn't feel inferior or anything like that. She was just astounding to me, with life and spirit in equal measure. Somehow, she could use the words "lovely" and "marvelous" without sounding pretentious. She expressed girlish charm in her wrinkly grin. I was impressed.

In my hungry way, I wanted to be significant to her. Oddly enough, I spent most of my time avoiding her.

I avoided her, because she had that unsettling power common to true conversationalists: complete, focused interest—in me. She asked all the right questions. Meg managed to provide the sort of stranger's vindication that a family never could.

Her interest in me made me punishingly self-conscious. I answered her questions, as if I were the village idiot.

Years later, I shared an afternoon hour with her, down the hill by the sea.

"Drop by for a bit of a chat," she'd said. We'd shared some flat pop and a bag of prawn crisps.

By this time, she'd become old. Her spark was missing. It had fled to the core, and that loveable personality was now blurred by habitual gesture.

Perhaps she was growing tired of herself, the nightly shows, two matinees on Tuesdays and Thursdays. The act was dwindling. There was no more Margaret Balfour.

My parents spent their hours speculating on her life. They discussed her eventual demise, the clockwork arrival of her mysterious nephew, and what would happen to the property. They talked of the house, as if it were their own.

iv.

Some people go on holiday by mistake.

My old mate Nigel came up once—only the once— late in the summer of '88. We were fellow grad students back then, thick friends, his city to my country, he a sort of Amis to my Wordsworth. But he was a wrong choice.

Being here turned Nigel into a regular builder, walling himself behind his reading, his thesis, and even his half-hearted beard. He had to keep the grass out, to put the lichens from his mind. He had to distract himself from all those inchoate things out there, calling ever so gently.

So, we dreamed of writing the great American novel. We shared the possibility of girlfriends. We hiked to the Old Man of Hoy, a dramatic stone digit poking from the Atlantic.

The day we hiked was fierce and amazing. The gulls hung motionless in the gale.

We spoke not a word. There was no evidence that Nigel was thinking at all. After a mile or so, he lit a cigarette, smoked it fast, and took off back to the car.

Later that evening, he returned to my room to play a single hand of cards.

v.

These were good times, though.

Take my 23rd birthday as an example. That was the summer I left for America. The family all came up then, for the adventure at the end of the world. Arriving were cousin Julie, her boyfriend Tom, Aunty Doris, and Uncle Bob.

The days were freakishly hot.

We all got so tanned that when people asked where we'd been, they shot back, "Piss off. Spanish brown, that."

We collected driftwood and laid a huge bonfire.

Mum built herself a sled from a fish crate, looped it with a hank of ship's rope, and loaded it full of the bone-weight wood. She dragged that thing for miles, grunting as it jammed between the jagged stones.

Dad scrounged up some long planks and half a dozen real wooden barrels, and built a camp in the snug of a horseshoe rock. In from the wind, away from the waves, it was a hideout that lasted for years.

There had been rich pickings, back then. This was all because of the Klondikers, the catch and canning fleet from behind the Iron Curtain.

Once a year they arrived, a floating city of five thousand East Germans, Bulgarians, and Romanians, packed into two dozen rusty ships that anchored in the Minch. They were hungry for toasters, tellies, videos, and jeans.

Ullapool cashed in, making more in that month than it did the whole year.

Mad Russian captains, hot on vodka, swam around their ships. There were rumors of Bacchanalian shore parties. Scores of lonely sailors whittled mermaids from their dreams.

Junk was chucked overboard. The bay was choked with their fascinating wreckage—coats, boots, life jackets, and rusty tins, with pictures of bold smiling fish, that nobody ever opened, not even on a dare.

Now, there is no more fleet and no more trash. Now, those beaches are pristine.

Oh yes, we had our bonfire. This was a massive roarer fueled by Uncle Bob, who was transformed that night from insurance man to a schoolboy, capering in his wellies. The sparks blasted high with every cured plank. The moon rose huge and blood red.

vi.

Twenty years later, Sue and I had our billet here. I must say that she was very brave. Three weeks spent in close quarters with the in-laws deserves some sort of recognition, even a medal.

We agreed to meet the parents down at the beach by the Youth Hostel. As they tottered off, we got a quick one in, the heat turned up between us. The possibility that they might return at any moment was thrilling.

By the time we arrived at the beach, we found them hunkering down in a lee. Mum was blue-lipped. Dad was poking into a tin of gluey beans.

Without prompt, Sue began scouring for sticks and ravels of plastic net. She roved up and down that chilly beach in her ill-fitting *anorak*.

"What's she doing?" Mum asked.

Sue knew all about the family myths. She understood the spirit of things and wanted to be a part of them. She got the bonfire going. Dumping on the wood, she cheered us all up.

Mum chased an ember to the sea. She was the happiest I'd ever seen her.

We played *boule* on the sand, each one landing with a wet *thuk*, like a disappointed cannonball.

vii.

That was the coldest June I'd ever known. There was no summer. The season failed to show.

In its place, a lashing Atlantic rain swept in. We sat in the conservatory, staring at our boneless reflections, the dead flies, the windows rippling in the constant gale. Morning turned into afternoon into night, as rain ran down the glass, filling up the fields. There were the usual claustrophobic irritations. Sue turned pages with an edgy snap, Dad furiously ground on his peanuts, and Mum would sniff suddenly, as if she'd been stabbed in the arse.

Me, I grew fond of the cooking magazines piled behind the toilet.

Between the pummeling rains, we managed to nip outside, in our desperate attempts to make this holiday a happy one. But even bundled up, it was impossible. There was no fun to be had with all that shivering. We clutched the burning iron *boules*.

Dad improvised an impressive lurching toss and landed his balls repeatedly on the jack. This was a move he'd seen a Frenchman pull off one year.

Nobody kept score, and in the tiny gap of glimmering sunshine, the midges came.

Scotland has flies, but the Highlands have their own savage gnats. They swarm in the millions, a floating cloud of blood-drinking dust.

Out they came—up the nose, into the ears, flitting around the eyes, biting.

Once, in the dread long grass at Slagan Bay, my mother fell into a midge panic, struggling, batting wildly, as they filled her mouth. Her look of sheer, drowning terror was unforgettable.

Now, as we fled, I noted two old ladies who were sitting on camp stools and calmly drinking flask tea. Their English faces were lost in a steam of midges.

viii.

Within the week, Sue and I took to our beds. We'd shoved together two of the singles. Because one was significantly higher than the other, we ended up with a mattress topography of hills and valleys.

There we lay, ignoring the flecks of sleet that hissed against the window. I sat upland, reading James Joyce. She curled silent below, reading Anthony Trollope.

That was my reckoning period.

We converted the middle bedroom into a writing studio, lugged the square card table up from downstairs, placed a bamboo chair before it, and plugged in an electric heater that had been clogged with fluff. There, I worked for three weeks, each afternoon shaping the novel I would actually finish. All was quiet, but for an aberrant cuckoo, but for my nib that scratched out the scenes.

Outside, the rain fell slowly, and all the world was featureless.

ix.

Downstairs one morning at 4:00 a.m., I made a cup of instant, took a chocolate biscuit, and settled into the captain's chair. The early sun reddened the distant mountains. Every mica vein, every scored ravine was visible. In that perfect peace, I vanished into something better.

That morning, I went for a stroll to the sea. I listened to the purple mussels suck and pop.

I found a patch of wave-flat stone and grooved to Roy Orbison's "Blue Angel" on repeat over my headphones. My feet found smooth rhythm.

His sad-but-hopeful voice quavered. Beautiful were the layers of doo-be-wah, yearning, breaking my heart. I saw myself in a movie, the opening credits rolling.

Everything had led me here. I knew that nobody had ever stood here, in this spot, in this precise way. I knew that I was making history.

As the ferry came in from the sea, I hoped that somebody was on deck, looking out with binoculars, that they'd see me dancing here, nudge each other, smile, and think me into their worlds.

When I returned, Sue and Mum were battling over their unspoken territory.

I nipped upstairs to keep my peace.

Sitting down to read, I accidentally cracked the glue spine on my book. Out fell all of those slithering pages.

Things really do fall apart, but not when you want them to.

Their voices came up through the floorboards.

Finally, Dad came to my room and begged me to intercede, since their disagreement was about my morning absence.

I think he'd been drinking. I think they all had.

I went downstairs and patiently explained why I'd left for the sea, and how I had struggled to return. They seemed placated, though more by my presence than my words.

x.

The village offered me a rich, true life. It was vaguely ceremonial, the way things were all in their places—the cows in the field, the gardener's barrow half-full of weeds, a bee caught in the net curtain, just off the verandah.

These empty rooms were filled with the ache of budding love, the perfect love of one who understands everything, who believes in me even when I can't, a love without all those slamming doors, without dishes clanking in the sink, a love with none of those patronizing comments, without those looks, without rain.

The days were clear and hot. Sue made us her special hand-flattened hamburgers on a throwaway grill. Everything was fine. We ate well. We had a few laughs.

Each of us was privately relieved that the holiday was finished.

Then, the days went strange.

Sue slumped down in her chair and began a meandering explanation of a heroine's desire, of the hero's casual acceptance of her cuckoldry, of his inability to change, because he preferred not to. She seemed to lecture less about her book than life itself. Her face looked like something off of a totem pole—smiling, impervious, leaning forward to inflict serious damage.

I blinked very slowly. For a terrifying second, I expected her to say, "I'm doing your dad."

Instead, she turned her hand in casual dismissal, and the moment was gone. So was everything else.

xi.

It's not ghosts I'm conjuring here. These mountains may be worn down to relative inconsequence, but they're still the oldest things on the planet.

It is 10:00 a.m., but it's broad daylight. There is a tinge of sickly yellow to the rain-heavy sky. I hear a trawler chugging on the sea, twelve miles away. The engine gears are turning. A spoon clatters on the metal deck.

No, it's not the ghosts I'm conjuring. I am summoning the gods of rock, dirt, blood, cold, rain, memory, love, loss, hatred, and suffering. I find myself at the center of my mind.

I'm walking, completely alone. The peaks are destroyed by fog. To my right stretches an ancient beach. There is not a single tree for shelter.

Out here, I'm an object in the landscape. I am without scale and slightly unnerved.

This stretch, from Culnacraig to Achduart, is scattered with lonely holiday rentals. From some, the tenants have long since fled, leaving their deep doorsills choked with driftwood and feathers.

There's not a soul on this road, today. I have known the occasional car, some driver who waves in acknowledgement.

There is nothing now but a sheep, huddling off to one side, grinding up its grass. It watches me through queerly reptilian eyes. It is waiting for that dangerous closeness. Then, there will be the explosion, the blundering into rocks and over the cliffs, the snapping of those twiggy legs out of sheer panic. Beside the sheep stand her lambs.

Oh, be still. Sweep down to the Minch, down towards those Summer Isles. Three electricity poles tilt, and a rusting machine stands just left of the bog. There is a stone outcrop, the cold, glacial rock precariously balanced.

Has anyone touched it, poked below it for certain treasure? I have. I've found a slug stuck to the quill grass, a fragment of urchin dropped by a gull. These are not exactly jewels, but they are what I've found.

Be still. Behind me, back towards Achiltibuie, the gloaming swirls around the lee of a mountain. My toes are warm in their socks, my kneecaps are damp against my trouser leg, and my voice mutters down the tunnel of memories. The future is no more certain than the hill hidden in the mist.

But the way clears. I glimpse Ben Mor, the long table-shaped mountain rising north and west.

Yes. This late morning, with sandwich in a bag and map case over my shoulder, I hike up towards the mountain's patient brow. I work my way through the tussocky ruts, hiding places to a thousand grouse. I'm carrying a bamboo cane with a hand-wrought silver top. It is beautiful, balanced, and a delight to hold. This cane belonged to Meg's father, and it remembers me.

The walking is tough. I follow the stream's flat bed. It rises steadily into a deep, fern-filled ravine. The walls are vertical, damp, and mottled.

I pull myself up. I am strong, invigorated by the view out across the Minch. Pausing for a breather, I touch Horse Island, squeeze Tanera Mhor between my fingers, catch Dun Canna in my hand. I think I could fly here—one easy step off the cliff and away.

The mountain rises simply, like stairs. There is the continuous upward hand-over-hand scramble, the call of muscles and sweat, and then, there is the peak. A sudden blast of howling wind flattens me. I am knocked onto my belly. Shale clatters off the ridge.

I don't care. In the rubble, a shiny beetle is busy with remarkable authority, clearing the way with his antlers.

I stand myself up to see where I am. The trail is the width of my boot. To one side, the scree curves down to the valley floor and to the home road. The other side is a sheer, dizzying drop of two-and-a-half-thousand feet. I feel only a slight twitch of fear.

Wild with new joy, I begin to run the entire length of Ben Mor's spine. Each leap is more certain than the next. My footing is true, guided. I cannot miss with my steps.

My hat sails off like a discus. Let it.

Utterly alive, I throb with my own tumbling voltage, shocked into the world, brimful of wisdom without any words. Then, the land is no more. I am at the tipping point. I have reached the silent peak of a stone pyramid. It is powdered with lingering snow.

I sit. I listen. Very slowly, the blue-sleek arrow of a British fighter jet banks below me. I look down onto the pilot. I see his black visor. I witness the red spinning light behind the cockpit. The burning fire of its engine silently streaks away. The roar trails seconds later.

This is the rooftop of my world. I would like to camp up here, to sleep safe in the clutch of that mountain.

But I never will.

Passing the turn in the road, I am almost there. The fog clears for Culnacraig, for home, for the last time. I see the derelict salmon farm, the fish long gone, the ro-ro container with "Rock Bottom Rentals" painted on the side. There is lodging for the backpackers who never come. There is the trail to Meg's cottage, then to our own. I see the conservatory.

Inside, my parents sit as they've sat for twenty years. She is reading in the corner of the lumpy sofa.

He dozes in the upright captain's chair. His book is butterflied on the tablecloth.

Every man has a door to heaven.

M. K. Meder

Spontaneous Shrines

They appear overnight,
at city crosswalks, curbs,
by a country roadside,

sudden *moradas*, altars,
without art or artifice,
haphazard and poignant,

plain white wooden crosses,
bouquets, wreaths of flowers—
freshly placed or faded,

bleached or bright plastic —
photographs, small flags,
religious figurines.

Think of simple people,
those who love well.
We drive on, admonished,

ever more vigilant
for any evidence
of the self in the other.

Lidia Kosk
translated by Danuta E. Kosk-Kosicka

AT THE WATER SPRING

I met you, Maria
at a pulsating
little water spring.
My pail was waiting
to be filled.

I kept meeting you, Maria,
whenever I needed
water from the spring.
When unsure, I kept
finding it, pulsating
in spite of everything,

and after years of
thirsting for its water,
if I traverse the distance
to find the overgrown path
and the hidden
water's eye,

the source
still not dried out,
I will meet you there, Maria.

Swami Parameshananda

LIFE FULFILLMENT

Every faith has its religious texts that explain how we can make connection with the divine or pure consciousness.

These texts can be read at any time, or in any place. Still, the masses choose to go to their places of worship. These places are conducive for concentration, due to the spiritual vibrations. They give a sense of fulfillment—fulfillment of duty, fulfillment of prayer to God. This act of sacrifice or *yajna* is an expression, knowingly or unknowingly, of the individual inner voice, or true self.

Bhagavad Gita gives a more appropriate and realistic explanation. Lord Krishna was lovingly goading Arjuna to pick up his bow and fight in the Mahabarata War. Imagine the chariot standing between the two armies, as all are waiting to start the war, this war between two first cousins. Here, Lord Krishna delivers the *Bhagavad Gita*.

In this *sloka* he is enlightening his favorite disciple.

> *Yajnaarthat karmano anyatra*
> *Loko'yam karmabandhanah*
> *Tad artham karma kaunteya*
> *Mukta sangah samacaacara*   *III.ix*

Unless work is performed as sacrifice, people lapse into bondage to their work. Hence, O son of Kunti, Arjuna, perform thy work as a sacrifice, shaking yourself free from all attachments.

The Lord explains that all beings seek to make life a fulfillment at three levels: competition on the physical plane, co-operation on the mental plane, and self-dedication on the ethical and spiritual planes.

Dhuryodhana, the one who initiated the war, was competitive throughout his life. Jealousy ruled his thinking to the extent that he tried to kill his five first cousins, the Pandavas.

In this, the lowest level of fulfillment, survival of the fittest is the nature of animal instinct. The weak are either left in the background or eliminated.

Human beings at this level are like animals. They eat, sleep, procreate, and think of security.

Take the bear as an example. The bear has an insatiable appetite. The bear sleeps for long periods, especially during the winter. The bear instinctively procreates, only at special times. Meanwhile, the father bear is protective of its territory.

Individuals with animalistic character, like that of the bear, make up the predominant masses of the population.

Co-operation is the next stage of evolution. Here animalistic competition is minimized. Competition is replaced with social life. Individuals look out for the interest of others by applying the universal law, "Do unto others as you would have them do unto you." In this way, collective peace and security harmonizes everyday living.

At this level, selfless service gradually destroys the ego. Performance of individual duties and responsibilities allows for collective progress and prosperity

Self-dedication, then, is the highest stage of life fulfillment. It operates on the ethical and spiritual plane. Only enlightened beings can practice self-dedication. They offer the best and most useful blessings for the welfare of society.

In the *Katha Upanishad*, the young boy Nachiketa demonstrates this quality. Nachiketa's father had wanted to give away barren cows to holy men. Nachiketa, however, vehemently objects. He asks his father to give him away, instead.

The act of giving without looking for anything in return brings spiritual evolution, both for the giver and the receiver. It is the essence of sacrifice, or *yajna*. Through sacrifice, the giver becomes further enlightened and prosperous.

For example, the giving of knowledge increases the capacity to teach; the self-dedicated person receives an abundance of divine knowledge and wisdom by way of God's grace.

It is this attitude of selfless service, or *seva*, that liberates one from the soul-entangling *karma*.

In the eyes of God, everything that happens in this creation is perfection. Human beings who act in the spirit of sacrifice attain this perfection, or liberation.

Lord Vishnu, the Lord of Sustenance, said, "I am sacrifice."

We cannot change this structure of competition, co-operation, and self-dedication. The great prophets or incarnations, like Krishna, Christ, and Muhammad, have manifested themselves from the all-pervading, pure, perfect consciousness to re-establish the balance between these three categories, so as to prevent chaos.

Lord Krishna in *Bhagavad Gita* says so very appropriately.

Yadaa yadaa hi dharmashya
Glaanir bhavati Bhaarata
Abhyuthaanam adharmasya
Tada atmaa nam srijamy aham   IV.vii

Whenever righteousness declines and unrighteousness thrives, O Bharata, Arjuna, I incarnate myself.

Paritraanaaya saadhunaam
Vinaashyaaya ca duskritaam
Dharma samsthaa panaarthaaya
Sambhavaanee yuge yuge   IV.viii

To protect the virtuous, to destroy the wicked, and to set righteousness on firm foundation, I am born and reborn from age to age.

Self-dedicated religious leaders need to be spiritual like this, meaning that they must manifest religious teachings in their lives. Their actions have to be what they teach. Then, continuous harmony of the house of worship will be maintained.

Furthermore, we have seen people become strong by diligently teaching religion in the private schools, especially during the formative years of children up to age nine. Places of worship that gear their programs for the benefit of the youth are building their future foundation.

Meanwhile, adults in the co-operative level must be put into leadership positions, so that they can be the connecting link. They are to persuade the lower echelon of the competitive masses to move up the ladder of God-realization.

The purpose of the human birth is to seek God-realization and universal emancipation.

It is inevitable that all will become liberated souls. This is the true fulfillment of life.

Contributor Notes

Carl Alessi is a self-taught writer and artist. Recently, his poems and stories have appeared in *Chiron Review*, *Outlaw Poetry Journal*, *Big Hammer*, and *Songs of Innocence*. His art has appeared on twelve covers of *Blue Beat Jacket*. His art has also appeared in two group shows put on by Art Enables in Washington, D.C. Much of his work is inspired by dreams.

Elvis Alves has a B.A. in religion from Colgate University and an M.A. from Princeton Theological Seminary. He lives in New York City and teaches at the John Jay College of Criminal Justice. His writings have appeared in *Colere*, *Tongues of the Ocean*, the *New Vilna Review*, *Heavy Bear* magazine, and others.

Gabriel Arquilevich's poems have appeared in *Notre Dame Review*, *MARGIE*, the *Wallace Stevens Journal*, *2River View*, *Numinous: Spiritual Poetry*, and other journals. He lives in Ojai, California, with his wife and three children.

Annette Barnes' poems have appeared in the *Hampden-Sydney Poetry Review*, *Stand* magazine, and *Plume*.

Stephen Booker was born on September 1, 1953. He has been on death row in a Florida prison since 1978. His writings have recently appeared in *Plume* and *Dorado*.

Felicia Bratcher lives in Westchester County of New York State. This is her first publication.

Dr. Edward Bruce Bynum is a clinical psychologist and the author of several texts in psychology, including *Dark Light Consciousness* (Inner Traditions, 2012) and *The African Unconscious* (Cosimo Books, 2012). He is a recipient of the American Psychological Association's Abraham Maslow Award. He is the author of several volumes of poetry including *Godzillananda: His Life and Visions* (Brutal Swan Press, 1996), which won the 2010 Naomi Long Madgett Poetry Prize. The present piece is excerpted from a longer unpublished work called "Confessions from the Earth." He is a *yogi* and lives near Amherst, Massachusetts.

Dietmar Busse, born in 1966 in Germany, is a portrait, fashion, and fine art photographer working in New York City. His editorial work has appeared in the *New York Times*, the *New Yorker*, *American Photo*, *Harper's Bazaar*, and *V*, among other prestigious publications.

J.J. Deur is a Croatian-American writer who lives and works in Brooklyn, New York. He holds a B.A. in journalism from CUNY. The theme of his work is often social and somewhat religious. As far as he recalls, he studied in a seminary, in a different part of the world, at one point in his life.

Joseph Dorazio is a prize-winning poet, whose poetry has appeared in numerous print and online literary magazines, including the *Spoon River Poetry Review*, Boston University's *Clarion*, the *Maynard*, *Sleet* magazine, *Nerve Cowboy*, *Philadelphia Poets*, and others. Mr. Dorazio lives and writes in Wayne, Pennsylvania.

Craig Evenson has been a third grade teacher for 28 years. His poems have recently appeared in the *Midwest Quarterly*, *Connecticut River Review*, *Sheepshead Review*, and *Sierra Nevada Review*. He lives in Northfield, Minnesota, with his wife and a number of other intermittently charming creatures. That's about the sum of it. He once saw Jesse Ventura in an airport.

Jane Galin lives in Portland, Oregon.

Franklin Gillette is a Colorado native, now living in the Bronx, New York. He won the 1998 Starr Symposium Poetry Contest. He has been published in *Poetry East*, *Aurorean*, and other magazines. He is also a librettist, painter, *yoga* teacher, and healer.

David Alan Goldstein has had more than forty short stories published in six countries. His writing has appeared in *Paris Transcontinental*, *Yuan Yang*, the *Prague Review*, *Confrontation*, *Evansville Review*, and many others. He is also a published poet. He was nominated for *Best Creative Nonfiction*, Volume 3 (W.W. Norton, 2009).

Samantha Haines is a recent graduate from the University of Tennessee at Knoxville, with a B.A. in English and creative writing. Currently, she is the founder and editor of *Glorydog Review*, a young literary magazine.

Paul Hansom's stories have appeared in the *Dickinson Review*, *New Letters*, *Chicago Quarterly Review*, *Alligator Juniper*, and the *Southern California Anthology*, among others. He has won numerous honors and awards, including a PEN/West Fellowship. He lives and writes in Ithaca, New York.

Dr. David James' second book *She Dances Like Mussolini* (March Street Press, 2009) won the 2010 Next Generation Indie Book Award for poetry. His one-act plays have been produced from New York to California. Dr. James teaches writing for Oakland Community College in Michigan.

Tayler Klein is a graduate student in creative writing at Pittsburg State University in Pittsburg, Kansas. Her work has placed in both fiction and poetry contests held by Pittsburg State University's literary magazine and a contest held by Kansas poet laureate Caryn Mirriam-Goldberg. Tayler plans to pursue an M.F.A. in poetry.

Philip Kobylarz lives in the East Bay of San Francisco. Recent work of his appears in *Tampa Review*, *Apt*, *Santa Fe Literary Review*, *New American Writing*, *Prairie Schooner*, *Poetry*, *Salzburg Review,* and has appeared in the *Best American Poetry* series. He is the author of *Rues* (Blue Light Press, 2011).

Danuta E. Kosk-Kosicka is a scientist, poet, writer, translator, photographer, and co-editor of literary journal *Loch Raven Review*. She resides in Maryland. She has translated two bilingual poetry books by Lidia Kosk: *Niedosyt / Reshapings* (Oficyna Literatow i Dziennikarzy POD WIATR, 2003) and *Słodka woda, słona woda / Sweet Water, Salt Water* (Astra, Lodz, Poland, 2009).

Lidia Kosk is the author of ten books of poetry and short stories, including two bilingual volumes, *Niedosyt / Reshapings* (Oficyna Literatow i Dziennikarzy POD WIATR, 2003) and *Słodka woda, słona woda / Sweet Water, Salt Water* (Astra, Lodz, Poland, 2009). Her poems and prose have appeared in literary journals and anthologies in Poland and in the United States. A lawyer, humanitarian, and world traveler, she has visited the United States several times. She resides in Warsaw, Poland, where she is helping to spread a renaissance of oral-history performance. She presently leads literary workshops and a poets' theater.

Lyn Lifshin's *Another Woman Who Looks Like Me* was published by Black Sparrow Press in October, 2006. Also out in 2006 was her prize-winning book about the famous, short-lived but beautiful race horse, Ruffian, called *The Licorice Daughter: My Year With Ruffian*, published by Texas Review Press. Lifshin's other recent books include *Before It's Light* (Black Sparrow Press, 1999) and *Cold Comfort* (Black Sparrow Press, 1997). For other books, biography, and photographs, see her web site: www.lynlifshin.com.

Rebecca Lilly works as a writer and has three collections of poems published, most recently a book of *haiku*, *Yesterday's Footprints* (Red Moon Press, 2012). A collection of her *haiku* on butterflies, *A Prism of Wings*, was published by Antrim House in 2013. Her author's website is www.rebeccalilly.com.

James Markay experiences poetry as the Zen of language. What makes his poetry come alive is that he is a man of no words.

M.K. Meder lives in San Francisco. His poems have appeared in *New Letters*, *Karamu*, the *Raven Chronicles*, the *American Poetry Journal*, *Pinyon*, *Mudfish*, *Rattle*, the *American Literary Review*, the *South Carolina Review*, *Peregrine*, *Oyez*, *Cutbank*, *Xanadu*, and the *HAIGHT Ashbury Literary Journal*, among many others.

Tara Menon is a freelance writer and book reviewer based in Lexington, Massachusetts. Her poems have been published in journals and anthologies, including *Aaduna*; *Yellow as Turmeric, Fragrant as Cloves*; *the view from here*; and *10x3 plus poetry*. Her fiction has been published in *Contemporary Literary Review India*; *Catamaran*; the *APA Journal*; *Elf: Eclectic Literary Forum*; *Many Mountains Moving*; the *South Carolina Review*; *Living in America*; and *Mother of the Groom*.

Rosemary Dunn Moeller has had writings published in *Prairie Winds*, *Common Threads*, *Encore*, and others.

Ayaz Daryl Nielsen is a poet, father, husband, veteran, x-oil-rig-roughneck, and x-hospice-nurse. He is currently the editor/custodian of print pub *bear creek haiku* (twenty-five years and over 100 issues). Collections of his poetry include *Concentric Penumbras of the Heart* (CreateSpace, 2012) and *haiku tumbleweeds still tumbling* (CreateSpace, 2012). His blog is www.bearcreekhaiku.blogspot.com (such fun). Considerable blame should be given to his having a B.A. in English from the University of Wisconsin—Eau Claire.

Barry W. North is a sixty-six-year-old retired refrigeration mechanic. Since his retirement in 2007, he has been nominated twice for a Pushcart Prize, won the 2010 A. E. Coppard Prize for Fiction, and more recently, won an honorable mention in the 2011 Allen Ginsberg Poetry Awards. His work has appeared in the *Paterson Literary Review*, *Slipstream*, the *Dos Passos Review*, *Iconoclast*, *Art Times*, *Ginosko*, and others.

Swami Parameshananda is an ordained *sannyasi* of Bharat Sevashram Sangha, a monastic and philanthropic organization with its head office located in Kolkata, India. He has lived in New York, New York for the last 30 years. He was handpicked and nurtured by the divine lofty ideals of Sreemat Swami Pranavanandaji. He is the author of *Eternal Answers* (Trafford Publishing, 2007) and *The Making of an American Yogi* (Trafford Publishing, 2008).

Leslie Plajzer is a retired parole agent. She lives in Baltimore, Maryland, with her husband and daughter. She celebrates 25 years clean in Narcotics Anonymous. Her writings have recently appeared in *Ascent Aspirations* and *Porchlight*.

Eve Powers' poetry has appeared in *California Quarterly*, *Rockhurst Review*, and *Purpose* magazine, and will soon appear in *Sufi Journal*, *Third Wednesday Journal*, *Hawaii Pacific Review*, and *Flowers and Vortexes*. Her awards include a first prize and an honorable mention in the National League of American Pen Women's Literary Competition, 2002.

Jim Richards teaches literature and creative writing at Brigham Young University in Idaho, and edits poetry for *Irreantum*. His poems have recently appeared in *Prairie Schooner*, *Poet Lore*, *Comstock Review*, *Texas Review*, and online in the *Fertile Source* and *Contemporary American Voices*. His poem "Horses for Hire," published by *Freshwater* in 2012, was nominated for a Pushcart Prize. He lives in eastern Idaho's Snake River Valley with his wife and five sons.

John Richmond has "wandered" parts of North America for a good portion of his life. Along the way, he has not only seen a good number of things but he has also lived with—for varying lengths of time—an equally good number of people. More recently, John Richmond has sequestered himself in his basement office, where he divides his time between writing and discussing the state of the world with his Doxie-Coonhound mix dog, Roma.

Elisavietta Ritchie is the author of fifteen books and chapbooks. Her collections of poetry include *Arc of the Storm* (Signal Books, 1998), *Elegy for the Other Woman* (Signal Books, 1996), *Tightening the Circle Over Eel Country* (Acropolis Books, 1974), *Raking the Snow* (Washington Writers Publishing House, 1982), and *Spirit of the Walrus* (Bright Hill Press, 2005). Her fiction books include *In Haste I Write You This Note* (Washington Writers Publishing House, 2000) and others. Ritchie's work is widely published, translated, and anthologized. She writes, teaches, mentors, edits, translates, photographs, and serves as poet-in-the-schools.

Stephanie Renée dos Santos is a fiction and freelance writer, and yoga instructor. She leads Saraswati Writing and Yoga Workshops in Brazil and the United States. Workshop practices are based on Kum Nye Yoga by Tarthang Tulku of the Nyingma Tibetan Buddhist tradition, along with Vedanta Yoga as taught by Sivananda Saraswati and Satyananda Saraswati, and the Amherst Writers & Artists Method. She's published fiction in *American Athenaeum* and *Lalitamba*. Currently, she is working on her first historical novel, *Cut from the Earth*. www.stephaniereneedossantos.com.

R.I. Sutton's fiction has appeared in *Kalimat*, *Zahir*, and *Cezanne's Carrot*, and was nominated for the 2010 Pushcart Prize. She lives in Central Victoria, Australia, where she is currently working on her first short story collection, *A Phantom of Earth and Water*. You can visit her website at: www.risutton.com.

Gabriele Zuokaite is a freelance novelist and poet from Lithuania. A high school senior, she is trying to develop herself as an independent contemporary writer. Her main topics are diversity, the suffering of being talented, loneliness, youth's aspirations, and incertitude.

ANAPHORA
LITERARY PRESS

anaphoraliterary.com
Submissions Welcome!

Pennsylvania Literary Journal

**PENNSYLVANIA
LITERARY JOURNAL**
(ISSN#: 2151-3066;
Library of Congress:
PN80.P46, 6X9", $10/iss):
is a printed journal that
publishes critical essays,
book-reviews, short sto-
ries, interviews, photo-
graphs, art, and poetry. It
is cataloged in the MLA
Directory of Periodicals.
PLJ has published works
by and interviews with
New York Times bestselling writers like Larry Niv-
en and Cinda Williams
Chima.

SPECIAL ISSUES:

**Popular Arts:
Volume V, Issue 2**
$10; 978-1-937536-49-7
Interviews with the *New
York Times* bestselling
science fiction writer
Larry Nivens and a Sun-
dance-winner, Tribeca
filmmaker.

**Reviews of Popular Fic-
tion: Volume V, Issue 1**
$10; 978-1-937536-46-6
Negative reviews of
best-selling novelists.

**Interviews with
Best-Selling Young
Adult Writers:
Volume IV, Issue 3**
$10; 978-1-937536-38-1
Interviews with Cinda
Williams Chima, James
Dashner & Carrie Ryan.

**Interviews with
Brooklyn Film Festival
Winners: Volume IV,
Issue 2**
$10; 978-1-937536-35-0

DISTRIBUTION:
• In full-text on EBSCO
Academic Complete and
ProQuest databases.
• On sale as single issues
on Amazon, Barnes and
Noble and most other on-
line bookstores.
• Baker & Taylor
• Ingram Book Company
• Coutts Information
Services
• Directly from Anaphora
with PayPal, Bank
Transfer or Check pay-
ments. Direct distribution
for orders of 10+ copies.
Email Director: director@
anaphoraliterary.com.

READER: You know our magazine is doing something different, something you can't find in commercial publishing. We're not afraid of literature, hybrid genres, foreign fiction, long poems, novellas. In these pages bold new voices appear alongside established luminaries, and the results are exciting, vibrant, literary. Be brave. Read adventurously. TLR.

TLR is one of the very best forums of new writing today. It strikes the perfect balance between formal innovation and human engagement… always stimulating, fresh, and smart.

– STEPHEN O'CONNOR

TLR

THE LITERARY REVIEW

AN INTERNATIONAL JOURNAL OF CONTEMPORARY WRITING

PUBLISHED AT FAIRLEIGH DICKINSON UNIVERSITY

SUBSCRIBE ONLINE.
WWW.THELITERARYREVIEW.ORG
$24 FOR FOUR ISSUES THAT'S 25% OFF THE COVER PRICE.
PREMIUM AND GIFT SUBSCRIPTIONS ALSO AVAILABLE.

PROMO CODE: PA2H

www.bluestemmagazine.com

bluestem

45130

SUPPORT REFUGE

P.O. Box; 131 Planetarium Station; New York, NY 10024

Lalitamba is in partnership with Refuge, a holistic shelter in New York City. Through years of working with people in need of permanent housing, we understand how stressful the situation can be. Refuge offers all the comforts of home to women in transition. *To make a tax-deductible donation to Refuge, please send a check to Lalitamba-Refuge at the above address.* Your generosity makes it all possible. Thank you!

www.threejewelsrefuge.org

SUBSCRIBE

P.O. Box; 131 Planetarium Station; New York, NY 10024

_____$10 One-year subscription (one issue)

_____$19 Two-year subscription (two issues)

Please add $4.95 for postage and handling and enclose a check written to *Lalitamba*.

Begin my subscription with issue number _____

Name_____

Address_____

City, State, Zip_____

Please send a gift subscription to:

Begin the subscription with issue number _____

Name_____

Address_____

City, State, Zip_____

CPSIA information can be obtained
at www.ICGtesting.com
Printed in the USA
FSOW02n0737270417
33614FS